TRAVELS TO MAYA

*14 Days
in the
Yucatán*

BARBARA MOULD YOUNG

Young, B. (2013). *Travels to Maya: 14 Days in the Yucatán.*
Pisces Publishing,
Olympia, Washington

Print Edition ISBN 978-0-9894430-0-5
EPUB Edition ISBN 978-0-9894430-1-2
Kindle Edition ISBN 978-0-9894430-2-9

Most photographs and all sketches are those of the author.
Cover photo: Historical site *Chich'en Itza: Temple of Venus* is in the foreground.
Temple of *Kulkucan* also known as *El Castillo* is in the background.

Back cover photo of author: Charlie Keck

Dedicated to

The International Committee

at South Puget Sound Community College

and Barbara Joslin Packard

Jon,

How special to get to know
you - again! Peace Corps Reunion
June 28, 2015 in Maryland.

Barbara (Bordwell) Young

PREFACE

The International Committee of our local community college hears my plans to visit the ancient ruins of the Mayan People of the Yucatán peninsula. Committee members urge me to consult with scholarly research books on our library shelves and with faculty who made the journey before me. Upon my return, I am to report to the campus community and am scheduled to lecture in the fall. Anxious to be well prepared, I take my journal for daily recording, my sketch book that I might better interpret what I see, and my camera to record people and places. For two weeks, I travel with my backpack by bus across the northern peninsula of the states of Quintana Roo and Yucatán, Mexico.

In the guidebook, you will note the spelling of Yucatán. Mayan scholars suggest the spelling should be "Yukatán" as it is closer to the Mayan language. I sense the possibility of connection of ancient Mayan Peoples with Native Peoples of the Pacific Northwest Coast and along the Columbia River where "k" is more often used than "c." To avoid confusion, I will use the more common spelling found in the tour books.

Chapter headings are the Mayan counting system of one to fourteen. The shell symbol is Zero. The dot is one. Two dots are two. The bar is five. Two bars and one dot is eleven. With a system of dots and bars, the mathematics expands. *K'iin* is the Mayan word for day. *K'iin* with the dots and bars takes you on a two-week journey into the Yucatán peninsula.

The Magicians House, Uxmal

Around the globe, people contemplate the explanation for the end of the Mayan calendar in December, 2012. It is my intent to share this trip with those who desire to understand a small piece of the Mayan heritage, culture, and calendar, and to savor the connections that we share together. I hope I can influence you to sling a backpack in place and join me on the journey.

BARBARA YOUNG
Olympia, Washington
January 2013

MAYAN NUMBER SYSTEM

0

1 •

2 ••

3 •••

4 ••••

5 ▬▬▬

6 ▬•▬

7 ▬••▬

8 ▬•••▬

9 ▬••••▬

10 ▬▬▬

11 ▬•▬▬

12 ▬••▬▬

13 ▬•••▬▬

14 ▬••••▬▬

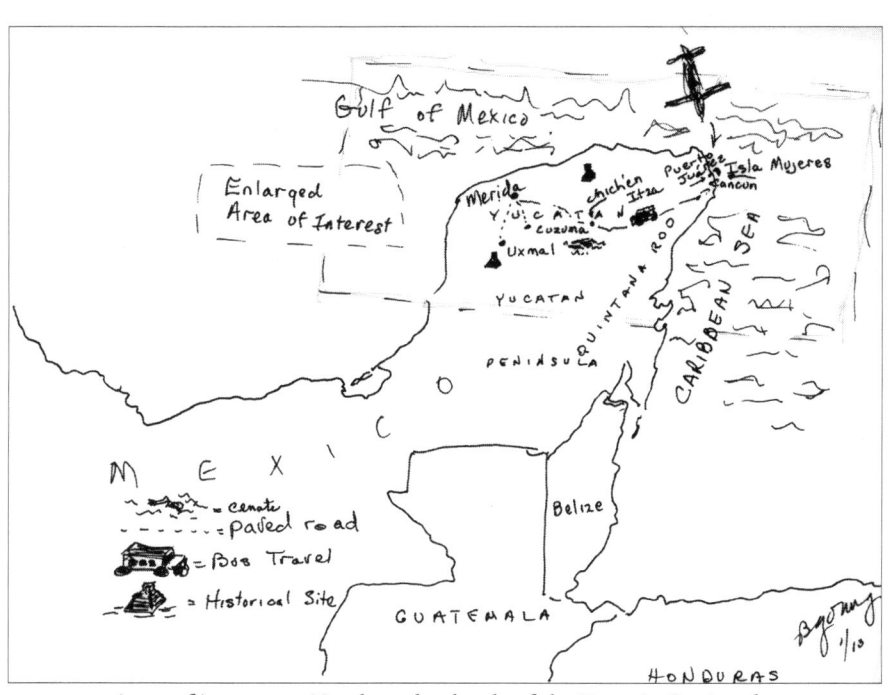

Area of interest—Northern lowlands of the Yucatán Peninsula,
states of Quintana Roo and Yucatán.

Sitting quietly, waiting for the departure of a flight to Washington, D.C. almost two years before, an airline agent announced on the loud speaker, urgently asking volunteers to give up their seat in exchange for an award ticket. Lulled out of my complacency with the promise of a free flight, I inquired, should I decide to be bumped. "Anywhere we fly," the agent responded and offered me three free flights for the exchange. Studying the flight map, the furthest point from Seattle was Cancun. Stepping forward, I took the bait, allowing the morning flight to leave with another person in my seat and the same night boarded the "red-eye," hoping that what I would lose in sleep, I might gain in travel before the year deadline came due.

———

Several months pass. I am determined to reap the benefits of relinquishing my seat. After grades are in and the current class has graduated, I select a date for departure and book a flight. This is my first summer break in four years of teaching psychiatric nursing and I am ready to travel.

Visiting a local bookstore and asking for a budget guide to Cancun and Yucatán Peninsula, the bookseller leads me to *Lonely Planet: Cancun, Cozumel & the Yucatán*. Glancing through the pages, I enter a world that is well known to those with budgets, backpacks, and laptop computers.

> *Ancient rhythms and customs form part of everyday life*
> *in the Yucatán. Women wear colorfully embroidered, loose-*
> *fitting huipiles (woven tunics) as they slap out tortillas in the*

yard; people live in traditional oval thatched houses, rest in hammocks after a days' work, and consume a diet of corn, beans and chilies (Lonely planet).

It is not just the distance that interests me, and it is not Cancun itself that is the subject of my destination. For many years, I have imagined walking among the ancient ruins of the Mayan people, well known for their advances in mathematics, astrology, and intricate and accurate calendar systems at a time when my ancestors were evolving in Europe. I pay for the book, take it home, and begin planning. I will travel alone, use buses between cities, and a ferry between the peninsula mainland and a coastal island in the Caribbean Sea—Isla Mujeres, or, in English, Island (of the) Women.

K'iin ●

A friend from the artists' group insists on driving me to the Seattle airport, about an hour's travel time. She skillfully deposits me at the departure door, gives a bear hug, and wishes me well. I wave good-by, turn through the automatic doors, and walk toward the gate.

My carry-on luggage consists of a light-weight borrowed backpack. It is without heavy frame, made of strong nylon, has cushy shoulder straps, and a broad waist cinch that fits snuggly on the hips. A new pair of Keene sandals from REI that accommodate my orthotics takes the place of heavy hiking boots and wool socks. It's going to be very hot where I am going. Waiting at the gate, my eyes drift up to the colorful window glass panels painted by Olympia artist Cappy Thompson. The panels cover the entire outside wall space of the terminal gate seating area, and I am drawn into the story depicted: a couple in bed dreaming of animals. As the flight attendant calls us to board, I leave the sleeping couple in their dreamland and step forward into the discovery of my own story. I am in the aisle seat exit row and agree to take responsibility in case of emergency. This extra room allows me to more easily stretch my legs and walk in the aisle. At some deeper level, it is as if I am a "wounded warrior" on a healing journey.

After a sleepless night flight to Atlanta, the first leg to the destination is achieved. In this busiest airport in the world and surrounded by a million people, I activate the cell phone and call my daughter who lives on the East Coast, knowing she is already at work. I give her a progress report. She offers advice: *Don't trust anyone. Don't tell people you are traveling alone. Tell us where you are. Send us your itinerary.* The flight is called for Cancun. As passengers carefully stow their bags overhead, flight attendants continue advice.

See the flamingoes on Progression Beach, said Raul born in Columbia.

Climb to the top of Chich'en Itza, said the flight attendant with short red hair. *If you get into trouble, I'll come and get you!* She was telling passengers the reason for short hair. *I cut off ten inches and sent it to the oil clean-up effort on the Gulf Coast. Hair is woven into making a barrier to the spill.* Each time the flight attendants move down the aisle offering water, I accept, feeling a bit of a headache and wanting to be rested and ready when the destination is reached.

It is a little before noon when I arrive in Cancun in the state of Quintana Roo, Mexico, and am stamped through the *Aduana*[1]. I enter a narrow hallway where three people are offering promotional trips that include discounts to see *Chich'en Itza*. I am curious about the offer and allow Alejandra to explain. I reply to her speaking Portuguese, hoping that it sounds a bit like Spanish. *Eu nao tenho interesse en sua condomiums mas tenho interesse in la viage ate Chich'en Itza.*[2] Alejandra seems to understand and says it is okay. For a small deposit (to show my commitment to attend) and for being willing to sit through a ninety minute spiel on the Maya Riviera, I have a place reserved for a fantastic buffet breakfast and a bus ride to *Chich'en Itza*. It sounds harmless enough since I have been honest about my total lack of interest in purchasing a condo plan, and it comes at the beginning of the trip which, I think, could be helpful for gathering information. I sign up, pay the deposit, and agree to be picked up at eight-thirty at Porto Juarez, on the mainland, the day after tomorrow. I continue my walk to the airport exit and bus stop.

Handsome new luxury buses wait outside the doors of the airport exit. The fare to the central bus terminal is forty-two pesos which is about four dollars in US currency.[3] The bus pulls out of its stall a little after one o'clock. I sit in a stylish blue cushioned seat, enjoy air conditioning, a sun screen on my window, and stare at a TV screen showing

---

1   Spanish for *Customs*

2   Portuguese for *I am not interested in your condominiums, but I am interested in the trip to Chich'en Itza.*

3   See Notes for exchange information between pesos and dollars.

something like Ninja. Prefer instead to look out the window to a landscape of white sand and palm trees. In exactly thirty minutes through heavy traffic, we pull into a modern, multi-windowed, air-conditioned, two-story, bus station. A line of taxis meet the bus travelers.

"Quanta o preco por la Puerto Juarez?" [4] I inquired.

"Ciquentos," [5] the taxi dispatcher replied.

"Vinte," [6] I said. He shrugged and walked away. Persisting, I called after his retreating figure, *"Donde pegar taxi for vinte pesos?"* [7]

"Avenida," [8] he called back over his shoulder, gestering toward the busy street to his left.

I rounded the building in the direction he had pointed and waved to the first taxi coming toward me. The taxi stopped. *"Quanta o preco por la Puerto Juarez?"* I inquired.

"Vinte cinco" [9] was the response.

"Vinte," I bartered. The driver accepted by pointing to the seat. I opened the back door and sat with my legs in the street as I un-cinched the waist belt and let the pack slide from my shoulders. I closed the back door and moved to the front seat passenger side. A lively conversation ensued, partly in Spanish, mostly in English.

"Alli tres desembarcaderos para dejar fuera Isle Mujeres," [10] he explained. One port ferries autos; the second port ferries tourists and working people. *"Alli une grande barco amarillo mas moderno por dosentos e cincuenta passajeros."* [11] This boat has room for luggage, has a deck on top, and plush reclining seats in the main deck. The second passenger dock is for the smaller, older boat built to carry thirty

---

4   Portuguese: What is the price to go to Porto Juarez?

5   Fifty

6   Portuguese: *Vinte* is twenty. In Spanish, Veinte is the word for twenty. The words are similar.

7   Portuguese: Where do I get the taxi for twenty pesos?

8   The avenue.

9   Twenty-five

10   Spanish: There are three ports to leave for the Island of the Women.

11   At one dock, is a larger, newer yellow boat, built to accommodate 250 passengers.

passengers and cartons of home grown produce on their way to market. Cost of the passenger voyage is the same for both the newer and older boats, about seventy pesos or six US dollars. I ask the taxi driver to drop me at the smaller boat.

I purchase a ticket and enter an air-conditioned room to join a crowd watching the world soccer games. As *Miss Valentine* comes into dock, a queue instantly takes shape. I take my place at the rear and walk in single file with the others. A vendor and her son load a large crate of beautiful tomatoes. The tomatoes look a bit like our Western Washington Early Girls only fully ripe. The passengers take seats on padded benches facing a TV screen that broadcasts the same soccer game we were watching in the terminal. *Miss Valentine* looks used and tired, but she gives us a pleasant thirty-minute ride across the water.

Disembarking and walking down the wooden planked dock, I am immediately in a different place—cobbled streets, small owner operated shops open to the street, walk- in restaurants open to the sea. The main street of town is a narrow boulevard that runs parallel to the shoreline and is lined with small shops. Parias, large cloth squares to wrap around the body as dress or skirt and very practical as beach wear, hang from rakes on the sidewalk. Touring companies tout their schedules. The pace of life and the language is less tense and hurried; the atmosphere is relaxed and calm. People are smiling and enjoying themselves. A Mountaineer friend, with whom I had conversed in the women's locker room at my local YMCA, suggested I visit this four-mile long, quiet, restful, get-away island community for exactly that reason— to unwind, relax, breathe in the atmosphere, and smile. A policeman stops traffic of bicycle carts and riders, just so I could cross the street. A man sitting on the back of a golf cart asks if I want to go on a snorkel tour. I laugh with pleasure at the question and teasingly respond, *"Sim, Senior."*[12] I am beginning to respond to the island atmosphere and feel calm, happy, and enjoying the relaxed exchange. Then, I thought more seriously that I might first focus my efforts to find the hostel. I asked

---

12 Yes, Sir.

the snorkel tour man for directions. It has already been a very long day.

"*Donde e el Calle Matomoros e la Hostel Poc' na?*" [13]

"*Matamoros,*" the man repeated, and thoughtfully considering the question, points in the direction up the boulevard—"*una, dos, tres, derecho hasta llegada o fin.*" [14]

I repeated, "*una, dos, tres, derecho hasta llegada la Hostel Poc' na. Gracias, Senior.*"

The Poc'na was the first choice for hostel lodging on *Isle* according to the *Lonely Planet*. The hostel, indeed, was at the end of Matamoros, with a sandy beach backyard between it and the sea. Entering, the open door from the street, the reception desk was across from a large bench. Behind the bench was a wall bulletin board which announced tours and activities. The entrance hall also had a small computer room which guests share. Beyond the computer, the hallway entered into a very large common room which served as a general gathering place for guests, dining hall, and TV room. This room had a thatched roof and was open on three sides with an entrance to the beach, a courtyard with blooming hibiscus, and stairs to second and third floor rooms. Poc' Na hosted a robust clientele. Although I had reserved the first night's stay, the receptionist reassured me that was not necessary; there was always space available. I gave my passport number, signed in for three nights, and was assigned to the women's dormitory.

Up an open concrete staircase to the second floor, turning left past the men's dormitory, I find the women's dorm at the end of the tiled hallway. The screen door is ajar. Entering a rather large room, I see four bunk beds, three lower bunks showing signs of occupancy. Two ceiling paddle fans and two oscillating fans stand on either side of the room. They are located between the bunk beds and stood out as necessary fixtures. I meet Nancy who is occupying a lower bunk and has a swollen

13   Spanish: Where is the street *Matomoros* and the Pocna Hostel?
14   Spanish: one, two, three, turn right until you arrive at the Hostel Poc'na. Portuguese is quite similar: une, dos, tres, directo ate o fin. English: one, two, three (blocks); turn right (and walk) until you reach the Hostel Poc'na.

foot elevated on a pillow. I select the remaining lower bunk between Nancy and the screen door, hoping for nighttime air circulation. Slinging my backpack onto the bunk, I realize just how tired and hungry I have become.

The Mayan women in the kitchen were preparing the evening's meal of three fajitas, salad, and choice of beer. My selection: Victoria. I eat only two of the fajitas and take the third one to Nancy. Her illness was due to a nasty sting of a jelly fish she stepped on in shallow water; keeping the foot elevated, she did not want to leave the room. Returning to the kitchen, I fetched an icepack for her injury.

I take my travel towel and walk to the communal shower, a small enclosure off the tiled patio two dorm rooms away and brush my teeth with bottled water. After returning to my bunk, I am ready for sleep, wearing as little as possible, stripping to the barest of coverings. Two overhead paddle fans are in constant rotation. Nancy and I put one of the oscillating fans between our bunks; its breeze rotates equally between us. Immediately upon rising in the morning, I will be taking shower number two. For now, however, getting through the night with the intense heat is my first challenge in island living, even though our room is open to the Caribbean Sea—just a block away.

K'iin ●●

At eleven o'clock the next morning, I place the small, around-the-neck travel towel, step into the hallway, and head to the common shower. A sign says to put toilet paper in the provided basket and not in the toilet. Okay. Familiar custom. We did that living in the interior of Brazil. You must not overload the septic system. I pull the shower curtain around the "L"-shaped tube rod and turn on the faucets. The shower power which might be about 14 streams, e *muito fraco*[15]. It is barely wet. Washing hair and body, I use as much water as needed to get wet. Turning off the faucets, it's hard to believe that I've actually showered.

I dress slowly selecting khaki pants, which I roll up to below the knee, and my light, white long-sleeve linen shirt with sleeves also rolled up, then, sport socks and sandals. Moving slowly, so as to not work up a sweat, I descend the stairs in search of breakfast and information.

Missing my free breakfast of toast, banana, and coffee because I didn't make it to the kitchen by 10:30, I order breakfast—croissant with ham and egg and fresh orange juice. Life is hotter and slower here. I wear no watch. A person takes time to converse, greet people. If you have a burning question, you

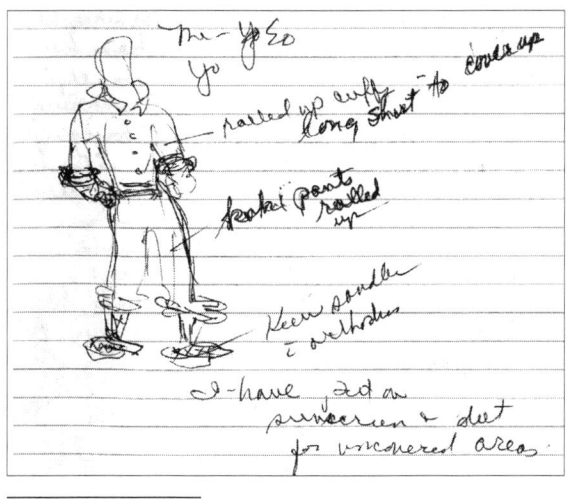

---

15 Portuguese: is very weak.

19

take your turn in asking it. One survives this heat by adapting to the environment. This is a small island community, and it is my first full day; I deserved to sleep in.

I observe who is saying what to whom and in which language. The hostel owners are Argentines. The students and back-packing travelers around me are speaking Danish, Swedish, German, Spanish, and English. The kitchen staff speaks Mayan. One thing in common among the guests is that they dress comfortably for island heat, carry backpacks which includes travel gear and lap tops, speak confidently and interact in an open respectful manner. My communication begins with Spanish/Portuguese. When that doesn't work, I try English.

As I consume my breakfast sandwich, I watch two different interactions going on around me. One is on the TV where the world soccer games continue; the other is a romantic intrigue happening in front of me. An attractive, dark-complexioned young woman is mopping the concrete steps to the second floor, the same stairs I descended just moments before. She glances over to the young man who took my breakfast order. The young man, the object of her interest has eyes for another—a slender young woman whose features have a less pronounced Mayan nose, a lighter chocolate complexion, who sits across from me on the other end of a long picnic-type table. Our table is on the outside of the common room, close to the court-yard. I watch the nonverbal glances and gestures as I journal.

Continuing to write, the sky darkens. Showers come, hard. Feeling a misty spray being blown in from the

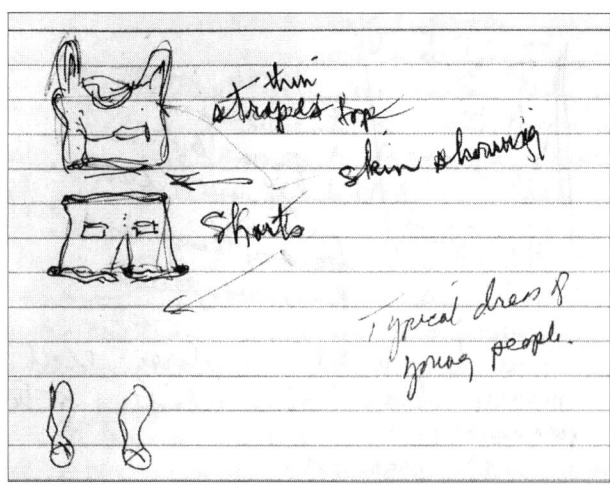

courtyard, I move from this outer table to deeper within the common room. The young woman at my table moves closer to the young man taking the orders and who is now sitting close to the front desk. After ten minutes, the showers cease. The rains have cooled off the hot environment, temporarily. Sunshine returns, and it is again very hot.

The young cleaning woman has descended the stairs with her bucket and is disappointed in her glance across the room to see her young man sitting and conversing with the other woman whose dress strap has slid off one shoulder. Another young couple, not of those I have previously mentioned, embrace near the courtyard. The heat and beauty of this place supports passion.

I must think of more practical things like looking for a bank to

exchange dollars for pesos. Plan for tomorrow. Shop at the vendor market across the street. Purchase a light cotton loose-fitting dress. Meanwhile, Greece is playing Argentina, and the common room fills to cheer on the "home" team. All rise for the Argentine National Anthem.

I want to ask the time and really don't care to know. What is time? It matters now only to catch the flight home. Acclimating to the tropical sun and island environment, I leave soccer match in play and exit the hostel.

As I walk through the streets, the sky darkens as if on cue, and the rains come again. *Esta chuvendo agora*[16]. The harder the rain falls, the more the streets fill with water. Darting in and out of overhanging awnings, I avoid the heaviest downpour. Arriving at the post office, I slip in out of the rain and buy stamps and envelopes for three letters. Walking in the direction of the ferry dock, I find the bank, exchange dollars for pesos, and set off in search of more adventure.

Cameroon vs. Holland. A shout rings out! Goal! Cameroon. An open thatched roof restaurant/bar at the port lures me inside. My table overlooks fishing boats tethered securely to their moorings. Relaxing, I order freshly caught fish in Mayan sauce served wrapped in a banana leaf, accompanied with fresh vegetables, rice, and *Dos Equis*. And observe ferries gliding in and out of the dock. Soccer action continues on the TV screen hung from the restaurant's rafters. Soothed by the soft voices of patrons around me, I am alone with my thoughts, my sketch book, and my second bottle of beer.

Final score: Cameroon 1, Holland 2. I have long since finished my second *cerveza*[17], sketched this scene, planned the next day's activities, and reluctantly prepare to move myself away from this pleasant place. A vendor of straw Panamanian-style hats moves among the tables. Failing to ask him the selling price, I tuck the thought away that it would be nice to return home with such a good looking hat.

Walking slowly back to the hostel, I enjoy the relaxed conversations between street vendors and tourists. Private home and commercial doors are open to the street to allow air circulation from outside in and inside out. On the sidewalks on metal stands, are an abundance of nylon/cotton *parias* for sale. A paria is a large square light-weight cloth used as a bathing suit cover up, an ankle length skirt, a short knee-length dress, a triangular wrap around the waist, or a wrap that

16   Portuguese: It is raining now.
17   *Cerveza* is beer (Spanish); *Cerveja*, (Portuguese).

is adapted for fashion and has a cooling effect in this hot climate. I see no *rebozos*[18].

Across the street from the Poc'na Hostel, vendors sell hand-made embroidered cotton dresses, T-shirts, hand-stitched cloths for the table, hand woven totes and handbags. An elder gentleman sits quietly on a stool by the street entrance, weaving and knotting the fibers of sisal and of colored cotton thread into strong hammocks. His fingers and hands move in a knowing practice that has been performed for years. I pause to watch him weave threads of natural and colored string into a stretchy length that seemingly could hold a great deal of weight. Hanging on hooks near where he is weaving are completed hammocks for sale, woven into varied patterns. He takes pride in demonstrating his skills, creating with practiced rhythm of worn fingers. I am mesmerized by the beauty of hand and finger movement and colorful outcome of intertwined thread. Language is of little importance. In silence, we communicate respect by honoring the art.

I walk farther into the market and look longingly over the lovely dresses, each unique in its pattern of colorful flowers, leaves, and border design. I select five items: a lovely blue/purple light cotton dress with colorful red, yellow, green, orange and white flowers carefully embroidered into a bouquet of flowers; a second dress of heavier cotton, all white with white embroidered hand work; a lovely blouse with embroidered sleeves; a little girl's white dress with sequins I thought perfect for my granddaughter, and a tiny white dress with colorful embroidery for the grandbaby, already four months old. I tried to purchase a dance skirt for my youngest daughter who would enjoy the flare during contra and swing dances. This skirt, of many layers, sown with a stiff polyester fabric is customarily worn by Spanish circle dancers. The selected skirt needs to be completed, the young salesgirl tells me, so I agree to return.

---

18 *Rebozos* (Spanish): a shawl, wrap, or scarf. My art teacher asked me to look for them. On this island, and in this heat, I cannot find them. The paria is the wrap of choice on the island.

The skirt was never purchased.

Back at the hostel, the viewers in the common room are riveted on the current soccer game—Slovakia vs. Italia, 3 to 2. Mexican music is playing in the background. Consulting with the hostel receptionist and wishing to be awakened at six the next morning, she demonstrates how to switch my cell phone from English to Spanish and to set the alarm. In the morning, I will sail to the mainland, be picked up at Porto Juarez as previously arranged for the condominium sales pitch, and be a guest for a Mayan breakfast buffet. I will learn how the Mayan Riviera is promoting resort life that continues to transform the natural beach coastline to hundreds of high-end hotels and to which the Mayan population of tiny interior villages are attracted as workers, leaving behind their traditional ways and transforming their ancient cultural heritage.

K'iin ●●●

Ringgggg. Six o'clock. The cell phone alarm is right on schedule. Quietly, so as not to disturb my sleeping dorm mates, I walk down the hall to the shower and return to put on my new purple dress, vivid color and light cotton. Before 7:00, I descend the stairs to the common room and ask the security guard to unlock the door. He points to his watch. Silently, we wait together. At exactly seven, the guard's watch rings. He walks to the front door, unlocks, and pulls it open. I sling my back pack in place, head to the port and buy a ticket for the seven-thirty sailing on the common ferry.

Arriving at Porto Juarez on the mainland at exactly eight o'clock, I walk the half block to the tourist ferry for an eight-thirty appointment with Alejandra, the lady who recruited me at the airport. When she sees me, she presents a small gift wrapped in paper. It is a tiny box molded of packed local sand. Alejandra hails a taxi, and gives directions to the driver for Mayan Riviera. Meanwhile, Alexandra returns to the airport to continue her recruiting.

The drive through Cancun is exactly one hour past hundreds of re-sort hotels with names like Hilton, Hyatt, Marriott, and Doubletree. Traffic is rushed, packed, tightly weaving in and out of *camions*,[19] cars, buses, and bicycles. We head south along the coast, taking the same road that continues to Playa del Carmen and the Isle de Cozumel. The taxi pulls into the Mayan Riviera at the same time as other guests are arriving. All has been prearranged and scheduled. I am transferred to a special golf cart and driven up a lushly landscaped circular drive. Our names are checked, and we are assigned a promotional partner. Mine

---

19   Trucks, small, compact buses

is a handsome middle-aged man named John, a transplanted Canadian who chose the sun and warmth of Cancun to northern Canada and chemical, environmental engineering. John smiles, relaxes, and escorts me to an incredible royal breakfast buffet—Mayan specialties, Mexican specialties, eggs, waffles, tropical fruits, Mayan hot chocolate, and of course, coffee. We may select from three beautiful long linen-draped steam tables, decorated abundantly with large vases of colorful tropical flowers. John begins the presentation while we eat.

After breakfast, we walk around the property which includes a surprise greeting by a rather large ancient-looking iguana on the stone wall next to the path. The swimming pool, constructed in three separate tiers, contains a large serpent statue with an undulating body which goes above and below the surface of the water. We visit guest rooms constructed with exquisite rare wood paneling, where lush, fluffy towels hang from bathroom hooks, and fresh flowers grace the bedroom. Visions of dollar signs flash before my eyes, and I consider how such a condo plan could be implemented on a single teacher's salary. I listen courteously, and say, "No, thank you."

My "no" response brings a referral to the supervisor and then the supervisor's supervisor. When I successfully work through the gauntlet, and my "no" remains unchanged, I am taken to a basement room where my deposit for the bus trip to *Chich'en Itza* is returned and am given a soft cloth beach bag promised by Alejandra. I can easily access *Chich'en Itza* on my own for far less than their planned discounted trip. My way back across town is not by private taxi but by group van pool which stops at the various hotels to discharge the "no" condo buyers. Departure from Mayan Riviera and the return trip past seaside hotels is not the life for which I had come to the Yucatán. My curiosity to witness this commercial glut is more than satisfied. I ask the driver to discharge me at the common ferry and am relieved when he does so.

Seven dollars secures my sailing with good, gentle, working class people. I sink into a padded bench and join passengers watching Spain vs. Chile. I look around at the predominantly chocolate skinned people with round faces and strong distinctive profiles, connecting them directly to the ancient heritage of their Mayan ancestors. Tomorrow, I leave the island and return to the mainland bus terminal to purchase a ticket for *Chich'en Itza*.

K'iin ●●●●

With the wind, the screen door of the women's dormitory banged against the waste basket. The receptacle had been placed in the doorway during the night. The loud clank awoke me. Reaching for my camera, I step out to the magic light of early morning. It had rained hard during the night, leaving puddles on the smooth tile deck. Through the palm trees, the intense aqua-green of the sea was visible. Waves moved with calm and eternal purpose. Walking down the hallway past the men's dorm to the open court yard, I glance over the railing to the street below and watch the weaver man across the street sweeping in front of his shop. Beyond him lies the uncluttered street—before voices and steps of humans replace the solitude. Turning toward my room, I slip on the wet tiles and fall as gently as possible, not to awaken the bodies in the men's dorm and not to damage the camera.

After I packed for today's departure last night while preparing for bed, I noticed my left ankle and foot were slightly swollen. I used my full pack to elevate the leg, and fell asleep to the artificial breeze of the fan I shared with Nancy. I am thankful that this morning, the swelling is down. Without disturbing sleeping dorm mates, I dress to travel, finish packing, strip my bed, and descend the steps to the front desk to check out. With time for a beach walk before my sailing to the mainland, I leave the pack with the receptionist and walk a sandy path to the water. Appreciating the aloneness with the sea, I pick up shells and pieces of tumbled glass fabricating stories of their origin. Absorbed in tiny discoveries, I ignore the familiar warning of darkened clouds. Rains come on their appointed schedule, hard. With pockets full of treasures, I hustle back to Poc'na and arrive dripping wet. This necessitates a change of clothes, so I dig into my pack for a solution. Wet clothes must be repacked and hung to dry whenever I reach the new location. I pack shells and glass pieces as well, adding extra weight to the pack.

Fully dry, I exit the hostel for the ferry dock, and still have ample time to visit dive shops along the route. Diving has been on my "to do list" since I completed a SCUBA certification 20 years ago in a limestone quarry in Houston. Good diving on Yucatán coasts and the reefs of Cancun and Cozumel has been well advertised and something to do before returning stateside.

Uruguay vs. South Korea. Those of us now on *Miss Valentine* watch with respectful attention. Exiting the boat on the mainland Cancun side, I ask the taxi driver to take me to the bus terminal for twenty pesos. He wants fifty. Not in the bartering mood, I cross the street and climb aboard the bus. The fare is five pesos and fifty centavos[20]. I try to give the bus driver six pesos to cover the fare. He would not accept the full peso and allows me to ride for five pesos. A young student asks to practice his English so we chat; he practiced his English; I, Spanish. We didn't have far to go, and I was grateful the student reminded me to get off.

The Cancun Central Bus Terminal is modern, state of the art with cushy seats in the waiting room. I buy a ticket on the second class Orient which leaves at noon, has no on-board bathroom, is air-conditioned, is a local—we stop at small villages along the way. It is a four and one-half hour ride to *Chich'en Itza*. I check out the bathroom on the second floor of the terminal carrying my pack up the flight of stairs. A guard collects three pesos for my visit to a clean maid-attended loo. Back on the first floor, I join the queue, appreciating the quiet time to study faces which speak to me of being present, comfortable, confident and unhurried, listen to conversation, and feel soothed by the tone and rhythm of the language.

At exactly 12:00 noon, I am motioned through the turnstile and climb aboard the Orient, selecting two seats together, one for me and

---

20 Fifty *centavos* would be the same as one-half peso.

one for my backpack. The air conditioning feels cool against my sweaty back, so I rummage in the pack for a light sweater. As the bus moves through the small villages, I feel as if I could reach out the window and touch the people we pass. Clearances for homes down narrow streets are minimal. I hold my breath as we come close to the corners of houses. In some spots, it appears that the ground has been eroded under the concrete sidewalk next to the roadway, making the existing sidewalk seem suspended in air. Cars passing the bus are so close it is difficult to gauge the clearance between the two. I am satisfied with the bus driver's steely confidence. This is no place for hesitation.

At precisely four-thirty, we pull into the parking lot at *Chich'en Itza*, and I am at once surprised by the Disney World-like crowds! At this hour, however, the ticket office is closing down for daytime visits to the ruins and selling tickets for the night light display on the pyramid, El Castillo. Two young men who traveled on the same Orient bus and who stayed at Poc'Na, turn to me for advice. *Lonely Planet* advises budget lodging at Pyramid Inn and they head down the road. It is Chich'en Hacienda for me.

The taxi driver quotes a fare of seventy pesos (about six dollars) which is more than half of what I just paid for a four and one-half hour bus ride from Cancun, and the Hacienda is just "around the block!"

"*Muito caro,*" [21] I exclaimed!

"*Sim, Senora concordo, mais...*" [22] He went to his taxi and brought back the published taxi fee list to hotels in the vicinity. Since this is a heritage site, fares of taxi service are determined by the government. There is no bartering. The taxi driver ferries me "around the block" to a cobbled circular drive of ancient stone at the bottom of a wide set of ascending steps, the entrance to 16th century Hacienda Chich'en. After assessing my appearance with backpack, the concerned driver asks me,

---

21 *Muito caro* = very expensive!
22 Yes, *Senora*. I agree, but...

"*ter reservacion?*" [23] Wondering if there were a mistake and instead he should be taking me to Pyramid Inn.

"*Tenho sim, Senior. Por une noite. Esse e lindo! Esso e marvelosa! Esta e bonita!*" [24] Reassuring him while paying the seventy pesos, I release the driver and walk up the steps slowly acting as if I am the Dona of the Hacienda. In the lobby, I walk past a large, round, wooden table holding a four foot high ceramic vase painted with pictures depicting classic Mayan life. I learn that quality reproductions and contemporary ceramic art comes from the neighboring town of Ticul. I pass the vase on my way to the concierge desk.

When planning for this trip, my nephew recommended one night at Hacienda Chich'en. I easily succumb to the quiet grandeur away from the tour crowd, appreciate the calm environment, and enjoy the birds singing in the garden. I pass on the eight o'clock pyramid light show at El Castillo, instead opting to move into my cabin, walk these refreshing and fragrant gardens, and swim in the pool under cover of tall palm fronds.

The cabins on the Hacienda were built in the early 1900's for archeologists who came to uncover the ruins. They have since been renovated for contemporary guests. The glossy red-tiled floor, colorful throw pillows with handmade yarn stitchery, and paddle fan are consistent with Hacienda décor. The modern shower, two full size beds and air-condition are appreciated by modern travelers in a hot climate. This is the right place to explore the mysteries of ancient Maya.

After moving into my cabin, I first hang up the clothes wet from morning rains, shower, and dress for dinner on the veranda which is freshly caught fish with a rich pleasantly spiced "Mayan" sauce and a local beer from Merida. The meal is expensive and worth every *centavo*. [25] With dinner comes a serenade—three voices, three guitars—and they

---

23 Do you have a reservation? In Portuguese, ask, *tem reservacão?*

24 I have, *Sir*. For one night. This is lovely! This is marvelous! This is beautiful!

25 In this case, *centavo* is slang, I suppose, for penny, as in, "It is worth every penny!"

sing to me. After dinner, I go for a swim.

Into pool, alone
Disturbance sends ripples to opposite side
Towering royal palms hover, offer enclosure
Stroking quietly
Gliding just below water surface
Lights under dark sky quilt dancing patterns
Like glass marbles of yesterday
Flipping the turn on far side
Emerging face skyward
Breaking through the water coverage

See palm frond bending, inquiring
Feel body sensuously stretch in backstroke rhythm
Smiling, thanking for their cover
Nodding to bending fronds
Gliding to corner pool steps, stepping out
Water droplets glistening on body surface
Leaving pool, complete.

In the garden, Hacienda Chich'en.

K'iin ━━━━

The Hacienda is one block from the south entrance to the *arqueological* zone of *Chich'en Itza*. I start the day with breakfast on white linen at the veranda overlooking the gardens and sculptures from the ancient city. Tropical song birds provide the background music for Mayan hot chocolate, fruit, and toast. In starched white jackets, the wait staff provides just the right amount of attention, and near the end of my breakfast, suggests that I take an umbrella from the concierge.

I walk to the entrance of this heritage park. There is no queue, having arrived before the ticket sellers. The entrance fee is 116 pesos ($11US). My International Teacher card is not honored here or at any of the Mexican sites and museums as promoted back in the States; only Mexican teachers can qualify for discount. Supporting this heritage site is as important as supporting the national parks in the United States. These incredible treasures must be maintained and preserved. Today, I will visit the grand pyramid known by its Mayan name as *Kulkucan* and its Spanish name of *El Castillo*, Temple of the Jaguar, Ball Court, *Temple of Venus*, walk the causeway to the sacred well, and then to *Caracol*, the observatory.

Chich'en Itza! I enter the sacred causeway, *sak' bej*.[26] A short way down the path is the first stone structure ruin, a small temple dedicated to *Xtoloc*, Lizard God. Just beyond the ruins, is the Xtoloc Well, where members of this early community retrieved their water supply. Original founders of Chich'en lived humbly in this area before the arrival of the Itza people under whom the community grew and for whom the community is named, the Itza being one of the many tribes of the Maya.

---

26   *Sak'bej* is white road.

Kulkucan. Standing on the edge of a large grassy field, I look across to the grand pyramid that represents this holy city and gawk with respect and awe. In Mayan, the name is *Kulkucan*, the Serpent God. *Kulkucan*, meaning feathered serpent is the largest and most impressive structure in this ancient city. The name *El Castillo* or The Castle was given by the Spanish or perhaps the archeologists who unearthed the building from its jungle entanglements centuries after the actual construction. The pyramid is also called "Snake Mountain" and is believed to be the place of origin and creation of the beginning of the world. It is a pyramid, has four sides, is 78 feet high and has 365 steep small steps to the upper platform. That is, there are 91 steps on four sides of the pyramid to equal 364 steps. The step to the upper platform makes it 365, the same number that is on the Long Count Mayan calendar. There are nine sloping platforms in upward construction. This building was built according to the Mayan study of the heavens, the stars, the movement of planets, and is a scientific recognition of the spring and fall equinox with the religious and spiritual celebration of the times of year. Author historian Richard Bloodgarden describes in his guide book a description of what the Mexican archeologist Luis E. Arachi explains as a most calculated placement of *El Castillo*. It emphasizes the spiritual connection with the Serpent God, *Kulkucan*.

> The Mayan astronomers so precisely placed the construction of this grand pyramid, that on the dates of the spring and fall equinoxes March 21 and September 21, a phenomenon occurs. "On the dark side of the main staircase, a series of triangles is formed which give the impression of an undulating serpent, descending in March and ascending in September. These serpent coils join the head which is at the base of the structure. This phenomenon lasts three hours and twenty minutes and is most impressive (Bloodgarden, R. 1982, p. 13).

Kulkucan/El Castillo

A large group of Spanish speaking high school students and teacher approach a good viewing spot; I hang out nearby and listen. Unable to hear the professor's lecture, I turn away to visit the Temple of the Jaguar and Ball Court and am lucky enough to be close to a five-member family group with guide.

Temple of Jaguar. The guide points to the stories explained in the friezes, chiseled into the façade and explains. This temple is built in honor of the God Jaguar, a symbol of power and authority.

The Ball Court. The group walks to the inner side of the ball court. I nonchalantly amble close. The guide teaches the meaning of the eye-level, playing field wall friezes—carved in stone is a description, a play-by-play of a pelota game in which one sees both the victors and the losers. The losers appear to have been sacrificed in their defeat. The victor in this game places a hard rubber ball through a small hole in a round stone ring which projects out from the tall side wall. The ring has been inscribed with symbols and is placed high in the center on the wall of each side of the playing field. Shields or yolks are worn to protect

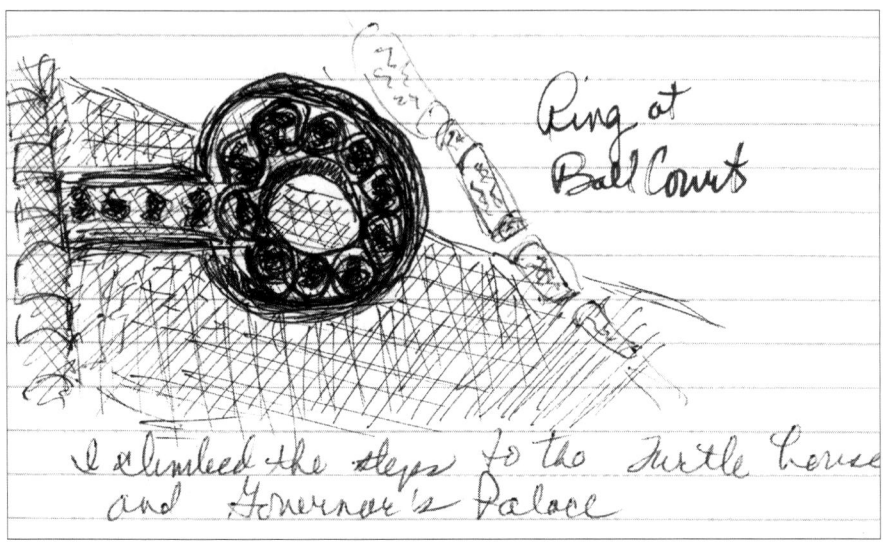

Ring at Ball Court

I climbed the steps to the Turtle House and Governor's Palace

the players from being hit by the ball. Linda Schele and Peter Mathews in *Code of Kings* describe this ball court as the most complex and largest of all the ball courts of Mesoamerica. This ball court at Chich'en is definitely Mayan and different from other playing fields because of the extremely high vertical wall and benches. Glyphs were the stories of what took place at the games played on this field and are the permanent recorded communication. Schele and Mathews explain:

> The ancient glyph... showed a cross-section of the playing alley. The stepped shape of the ball court glyph reflects its definition as the crack in the top of the Creation Mountain. In the Popol Vuh of the K'iche' Maya, hom, "crevice" is the word for "ball court." As a crevice in the surface of the earth, the ball court gives human beings access to the Otherworld, where the gods and the ancestors live. For the Maya, to play the ballgame was to bring back the moment when the Third Creation ended and the Fourth one began.
>
> At *Chich'en Itza*, this hom, or "crevice," in the earth has a wall enclosing the playing field so that the ballgames could not be viewed by large audiences. The games played there

38

were not sport, but deadly serious affairs involving the charter of the state and communication with the Otherworld.

The imagery associated with the structures of the ball court and surrounding buildings records the critical moments in the city's history—what happened to the ancestors of the Itza at the moment of Creation and the founding of their city and what happened during the wars of conquest that gave the Itza their right to rule. The Creation imagery of the two critical domains of statecraft is described—the sacred art of warfare and sacrifice, and the role of the ballgame in the passage of authority from generation to generation through rites of accession (Schele, L. and Mathews, P. p. 207).

As I listen to the guide explain these glyphs, these stories in stone of Mayan life, I am also pulling my rain jacket out of my pack and preparing for what appears to be an approaching shower.

The boundary of the ball court is defined by the Temple of the North and the Temple of the South. Acoustics are so precise here that a person can sit on a bench at the Temple of the North and be heard by a person sitting at the Temple of the South, as if the people were conversing side by side. The distance between the two locations is 460 feet.

Leaving the ball court on the north end, the small group next visits the Trompantli, a platform building which has a panel of skulls. It is believed that this building was influenced by the Toltec, a Mayan clan who inhabited this community following the Itza people and brought to the city its influence and beliefs of war and death.

Temple of Venus. Walking back across the field to the north of the pyramid, one faces the Temple *of Venus*. Large serpent heads with open mouths were carved into the four staircases of the temple. To the rear of the temple is a stairway of un-restored rock, and, at ground level, a reclining figure of Chacmol. The lap of Chacmol looks suspiciously like it could be a place of execution.

Across from the temple is a long relief panel of jaguars in a stage of restoration. The panel was previously attached to the façade of a building, probably having to do with the Temple of the Jaguar. To protect the long panel from the rain, a roof of palm fronds had been constructed and placed over the entire length. It is the same construction of natural material for roofs seen on the homes in the small villages that my bus almost touches in its movement through the towns.

Cenote Segrada.[27] I move onto the causeway, another sak' beh,[28] constructed with a foundation of white stone, in a straight trajectory, directly connecting Kulkucan, *Temple of Venus*, and the Sacred Well. Along this path are now modern day merchant tables selling modern day tourist items. I am distracted from my mission and stop to admire the Mayan calendar T-shirt. Remembering my focus along the sak'beh, my attention returns to the destination; I continue on the path to see and understand the reason for pilgrimages of the faithful to the sacred well.

It is *Cenote Segrada* in Spanish; Ts'ono'ot, in Mayan. The sacred well is also the Well of Sacrifices and was used for ceremonial purposes to honor the Rain God Chaac. Pilgrims would come to this well from modern day central Mexico, Honduras, Costa Rica, Guatemala, Panama, and Colombia, and even the southwest of the United States (as evidenced by the turquoise that was recovered from the well). The time frame of these pilgrimages is thought to be dated from the 13th to the 16th centuries which would put this after the decline of the Itza community at Chich'en. The bottom of this well is covered with mud and silt which protected many found objects of gold, jade, copper, shell, stone, and wood. Human skulls have been recovered as well. The ruin of a steam bath is located on one side of the well and is thought to have been used for purification rites before the sacrifice. This is an open well of deep green color due to the vegetation matter at the bottom. The well is round in shape, seems partially man-made and has a diameter that

27   Spanish for Sacred Well
28   Again, *sak'beh* is white road.

measures 65 yards. From rocky ledge to water level is calculated to be 72 ft. The depth of water continues for another 40 feet.

Peering down into the well, I wonder about those who were sacrificed here: warriors, children, young virgins with jewels and of the rich offerings sent with them, and if it were enough to please Chaac and deliver the needed rains. The recent shower was refreshing, refolding my rain poncho, and replacing it into my pack.

Cenote Segrada

Mexico vs. Argentina. Mexico just made a goal! Cheers go up Spectators cheer. A huge crowd of tourists, staff, and vendors crowd around the only television set.

The book store, located beyond the TV crowd is my next stop—to purchase Mayan stories for grandchildren, and talk with the representative of the bus company concerning the schedule for tomorrow's travel to Merida. Carocol, the ancient observatory, is next.

Caracol. Strolling along the dirt and stone path, I found myself enmeshed in a rather large group of tourists led by a handsome, animated, and enthusiastic Tour Guide Simon Chavez Flores, no. 04073. Some of those in the back of the group were barely listening and seemed not to care, so I move closer to the front where an assertive woman is asking interesting questions in English. Intensely focused in historical Mayan culture, Sr. Flores must be an anthropology professor of the local community college.

> "The observatory was one of the most important structures in the sacred city of the Itza. It was built for the Maya astronomers to study Venus, the heavens, and the stars and supported their continuous explanations of creation and death, of beginning and ending, of the seasons and when to plant the corn." Simon went on to explain the cylinder building on top of the double platform. It is unique. The parapet on top, with windows placed to face each of the cardinal directions, was accessed by a circular staircase. The name Caracol means "the snail" describing the staircase."

We walked quickly across the field to visit the Deer House, named for a relief of a deer on its façade; the Red House, painted with enduring red paint; the Church, which I learned was an excellent example of Chenes style architecture, and the Nunnery, an example of the Classical Puuc-style architecture. Sr. Flores continued.

> "Chenes is the intricate stone design over the top and bottom of the façade of the building and the name is taken from the region in which it was first introduced. Classical stands as the pinnacle of the Maya civilization in terms of its exquisite architecture, art, and living, a period which is dated to about 900 BC to 900 AD. Puuc-style comes from the Puuc area of the central northern Yucatán peninsula and describes the intricate stone facades on the top of the building leaving the bottom façade without decoration."

"Puuc" is Mayan for hill. Receiving the English translation of these architectural styles made my head spin, and I thought of my American nursing students trying to remember the list of symptoms attached to various diagnoses on the Diagnostic and Statistical Manual (DSM).

The guards are hustling us toward the main entrance for closing. Walking beside the guide and wanting to test my theory that he is a college professor on summer break, the assertive lady asks instead. Flores is not a college professor; he is a certified, tested, and examined official tour guide for the heritage park. The lady gave him a handsome tip which alerted me to do the same. Sr. Flores told me privately he did not need to teach school and that he was well paid as a tour guide. *"It was an important job to help others understand their heritage and for us all to be sensitive to the unique contribution of cultures. When we truly listen to the lessons of the ancient peoples, we can learn to live more fully, connected with the purpose of our creation."*

Separating from the group, I take the path to the east entrance. My tired feet are starting to ache, but with thoughts of the hacienda, warm food and a cool swim, my feet pick up the pace, focusing on the environment: a tall tree whose roots had grown around and down the side of a house much like the nurse logs of our Pacific Northwest, and a brightly blooming, red, hibiscus bush along a cobbled stone path.

Ascending the ancient pale clay-colored steps of the hacienda front entrance which I had first climbed only the evening before, I return the borrowed umbrella to its can by the concierge desk, walk through the open lobby feeling the cross breezes from the inner garden, and take notice of the eloquently set white linen tables ready to receive guests for dinner. Down the garden steps to the red brick walk to my cabin, I unlock the door and sigh with relief, pleasure, and a great deal of satisfaction.

Deciding on a swim before dinner, I am not alone. A nice man begins to speak to me in German, assuming I am a member of a group that has recently arrived. I consider what he is saying, but having been forty years since my German lessons, I respond in Portuguese. Completing the swim, I dress for dinner. Shannon, a teacher from California who occupies the duplex part of the cabin, joins me for a beer on our common porch facing the garden. In large wicker, amply cushioned chairs, we recap the day's adventures, then, take the same redbrick walk to a pleasant dinner on the main veranda.

A Toltec structure, *Tzompantli*, (Axtec meaning skull platform),
Chich'en Itza (Bloomgarden)

K'iin ___•___

Awaking to an air conditioning motor hum competing with tropical song birds, the birds win. I open the screens and windows to my paradise retreat. Today, I must say good-bye to Hacienda life. Believing the water is healing, I shower, take my medicines with bottled water, apply sunscreen, Deet, and tiny bit of make-up, focusing on the eyes. The Mayan women are so conscious of beauty and with the emphasis on the eyes. Making bandages for sore toes, I dress, roll clothes, and tuck into the pack, not in a hurry to leave. For all my frugality and bragging about getting by on a lean budget, I allowed myself to be pampered in the Hacienda environment. Feeling no stress, I listened to the birds. This stay helped me gain a balance, a harmony with life. As the ancient Mayans believed, this is the creation of a new day.

Shannon greets me as I exit my room and we go for coffee. Instead, I request Mayan hot chocolate while we chat of royal palms, gardens, air plants on trees, ancient stones, Mayan columns, and history. When Shannon leaves to visit a small hacienda church, I depart for the east gate park entrance, planning to walk through the park to the bus stop in front of the main visitor's center.

Without a paid daily pass, the guard stops me, and I explain to him. *"Eu estava aqui ontem para visita Chich'en. Donde pegar o omnibus por Merida? He understands my question and purpose."* [29]

"Para la," [30] pointing in the same direction that I was heading. He waved me through the entrance gate onto the *sak'bej*. In the area of *Kulkucan*, a lady approaches, asking me to buy her handmade embroidered clothes; I purchased two and ask if I might take her photo, giving

---

29 Portuguese: I was here yesterday to visit *Chich'en Itza*. Where do I get the bus for Merida?
30 Portuguese: Over there.

her an additional two pesos.

The ticket on the second class bus to Merida for 63 pesos ($6US). Sitting on the curb with my backpack firmly strapped in place, I watch the park workers arriving. When my bus pulls in, I ask the nicely dressed ticket man to help me get to a standing position. Trying to show his strength, he smiles, and extends his hand. I rise to my feet and board the bus. I select two seats close to the front. Unhooking my hip belt and chest straps, I let my backpack fall into the aisle seat while I sit by the window. *Lonely Planet* is opened to Merida—its history, culture, and most importantly, where to find the night's lodging. Sitting comfortably in the cooled air of the bus, I am untouched by the steamy, humid, jungle environment outside my window. Bus driver takes the bulky bus down narrow streets of tiny villages where homes are modest, square, open-door, with palm leaf thatched roofs. Political signs are attached to poles, house fronts, anywhere they can be stapled; It is getting close to election day. Watching the sky turn dark, the rains come.

It is a heavy downpour as we enter Merida and the bus sloshes through flooded intersections. People retreat inside shops. Disembarking from the bus and left alone at the station, I feel disoriented in the downpour and wish to find lodging. *Lonely Planet* describes my selected destination of Hostel Zocalo: *"a great location and beautiful old colonial building... located on one of the nicest plazas in Mexico... El Centro is where laurel trees shade the sidewalks and pedestrians make this a busy, central meeting, shopping, and church gathering place."* Hostel Zocalo sounds like a dry shelter where I can find company. I duck into a furniture store to have the owner help me understand the street map to the Grand Plaza.

The sudden rains are so dense that most inner-city intersections have flooded. I back up several paces to find higher ground to cross the street. This rain is the result of hurricane-force winds that had threatened the eastern side of the peninsula. Three days ago, when I was using the free computer at Hostel Poc'Na on Isla Mujeres, my sister had sent an e-mail and inquired concerning the hurricane warnings. At that time, I was not touched by the threat and didn't know about the report. In the next communication, I can report wet feet from fording flooded intersections. A wonderful, warm, nonverbal, cross cultural communication occurred during this search for "higher ground."

A well dressed Mayan lady vendor was sitting under the canopy on one of the flooded street corners. I was looking for a less-deep-water place to cross. I looked up to catch her eye, shrugged my shoulders, as if to say, *Oh well, I am trying to find higher ground in this deluge.* She responded by smiling, rolling her eyes to the sky as if to say, *Oh well, that is the way it is.* Feeling a human connection and an understanding of life's challenges, I laugh and enjoy the humor.

Hostel Zocalo is located in a 16th Century Spanish Colonial building facing the central plaza. Beyond the fifteen foot, heavy, sturdy doorway, I climb the circular stairway of marble steps and wrought iron railing to the second floor. Urina is at the desk and shows me the women's dormitory just off the open courtyard hallway. It is crowded with bunk beds. I ask to see private accommodations and am offered a room between the kitchen and the house manager for 200 *pesos* per night ($20US). It is an interior room, has a very high ceiling with a paddle fan. I like the privacy part to arrange my things and lock the door when leaving the hostel. It is a bit stuffy, not being directly on the open air courtyard, but I can survive with the help of the paddle fan. I pay $M600[31] for the anticipated three nights' stay. Stowing my pack, I return to the street to look for a bank to buy pesos.

Half way down the spiral marble staircase, estimated to be about fifteen deep steps under the second floor lobby, is tucked a small mezzanine, containing several computers for hostel guests. The fee is 10 pesos per half hour, about one dollar. I email family that I am safe, comfortable, and barely touched by the storm for which they were concerned. Descend the remaining steps to the first floor, I exit to the plaza. Street vendors sell sausages and sweet pastries. Drug stores, shoe stores, dress stores, and groceries, I pass all on my way to look for a bank. About

---

31   $M600 is the same as 600 pesos. The "M" is for Mexican. Throughout the text "M" and "US" can be interchanged with pesos and dollars.

three blocks from the hostel, I find a Banco Azteca and exchange 100 US dollars for 1, 206 Mexican pesos. Flush, I return to the Grande Plaza and look for an open café to observe this hour of *passeando*.[32]

Opposite the cathedral, I find a table under the colonnade in a pleasant open-to-the plaza café and order *cerveza*, a large plate of nachos and guacamole, and retrieve my journal. Since my table is closest to the street side, I am interrupted frequently by strolling vendors wanting me to purchase colorful bags, hammocks, and blouses. A small table is arranged almost inside the restaurant where I can observe and write with fewer interruptions. With a second *cerveza*, I sit for three hours, long enough to sketch dad, mom, and son who occupy the next table; long enough to record in my journal; and, long enough to see the placement of chairs, a stage and dance floor set up next door for a free evening of music.

As the sky turns into evening, the set-up chairs down the colonnade next to the café are filling. I close my journal, pay my check, and move. Selecting a seat near the outside in a slowly filling row, I watch an attractive older woman gracefully walking among the rows selling sweet cakes from her basket. She is wearing the traditional white Mayan loose fitting cotton dress over an undershirt of lace. To this is added a brown and white woven *reboza*[33] draped dramatically around her shoulders.

> Weathered face
> White hair thin
> Slight in stature; yet
> Standing tall;
>
> Holding basket of wrapped *doces*[34]
> Moving among chairs
> Asking the waiting to buy her treats;

---

32   The Portuguese verb *Passear* is to take a walk, to promenade. *Passeio* is a masculine noun for walk, promenade. *Passeando* is the process of walking to be seen in the plaza in the evening, often the time the young girls want to be noticed by the young men and vice versa; a time to be seen; a time for flirting.

33   Spanish for scarf, cape. I found this particular style work by prominent vendor ladies.

34   Portuguese: *doces* are sweets. In Spanish: *dulces* are sweets.

Brown and white *reboza*
Drapes around her neck
Signifying importance of her business
presence, wisdom;

Sensing her spirit
Dignified
Proud;

Glad for her existence
Nourished by her hand work
Calmed by her presence.

A nice looking gentleman selects the empty seat to my left. He leans toward me and asks if he might practice his English. *Sim,*[35] exchanging my English for his Spanish. When the promised live music has not yet begun, and feeling exhausted from the loud, canned, prerecorded music, I excuse myself. Hoping that the man was truly at the concert for the concert, I cross the street in front of the *palacio,* take a circular route to my hostel on the south side of the plaza, climb the marble steps, and enter a large, unoccupied guest room which opens onto the plaza. Siting on the balcony with scrolled wrought iron grill work partially concealing my presence, I look down upon musicians warming up their guitars and drums for their turn at performance. I have my own serenade below the balcony window. Around nine o'clock, the stage music begins and drifts upward to where I am listening. Later, tiredness overtakes me and I retire to my private bedroom.

Passing the Reception Desk, Urina says *Ola. Boa noite. Hasta manana.*[36]

Hasta manana. Closing the door of my private room, I lay down with feet elevated on pillows, paddle fan purring, and hoping swollen ankles will be less obvious by morning.

---

35 Portuguese: yes

36 *Ola* is a Spanish expression used as a courtesy when you are about to engage in conversation. It is an introduction like, "Excuse me, ..." *Boa noite* is Portuguese, "Good night." *Hasta manana* is Spanish, "Until tomorrow." I combined these languages because they fit the purpose and sounded right.

Well-dressed merchant with *rebozo*, Merida

K'iin ▬●●▬

After a delicious breakfast of papaya, mango, banana, cheese, yogurt, toast, eggs, and ham that Oscar, the day manager, put out on the common table by seven, I was ready to review with Urina, a few of the common Mayan words I had seen in brochures, on signs, and posted behind her desk. As she spoke, I took notes in my journal.

Ajaw, pronounced "ah how?" is ruler, leader.

Cho co late is the Mayan drink. *Cho co* means chocolate. Late means careful. Be careful when imbibing this hot drink.

Quetzal is a bird whose feathers are highly prized and these feathers are symbols of power worn by a Mayan leader.

Coatl means snake.

Quetzalcoatl is also the name of a leader of the Toltec. The name became the name of the Serpent God and is thought to have come originally from Central Mexico and could have been Toltec or Aztec.

Kukul is the Mayan name for feathers.

Can means serpent.

Kulkulcan is the plumbed (feathered) serpent, the most powerful Mayan God and the name given to the grand pyramid of *Chich'en Itza. Kulkulcan* is the plumbed serpent seen on the temples of the most important rulers.

Chicle is the chewing gum tree.

Tumkul means drum

Chac is red.

Mool is claw.

Chaac is the Rain God; chaac is the rain.

Itzamna is knowledge.

The sign of the X in a box is the symbol of nobility and of rulers.

Gracias in Spanish is *dios bo' otik* in Mayan.

I have been given just enough information to know that my Portuguese Spanish does not get me far in a state where 39% to 69% of the population in small rural villages continue to speak their Mayan dialect. Urina urges me to "hit the streets" and try out my sparse Mayan vocabulary. I descend the marble staircase.

A free guided tour of the historic center focusing on Plaza Grande will depart at 9:30 in front of the Palace Municipal. When I arrive, another couple wanting the same tour in English is waiting. Our tour guide begins.

> *El Centro is Grande Plaza and always bustling with pedestrians crossing to and from the park. It was the religious and social center of ancient T'ho, a strong impressive tribe of Maya with temples facing the central park. With the Spanish conquest of the Mayan tribes, the community of T'ho disintegrated. The stones of the Maya temples were pillaged and used for the construction of Spanish buildings which now stand on four sides of the plaza. The Mayan temples were replaced with the current colonial buildings whose integrity the city has promised to protect. Attempts to change this colonial character have been met with resistance.*

On the East side of the plaza is the imposing, tall stone *Cathedral de San Ildefonso*. Construction took 37 years. A massive crucifix behind the altar is *Cristo de la Unidad* or Christ of Unity, symbolizing the reconciliation between the Spanish and Maya heritages as depicted from the perspective of the Spanish Bishop. Within the cathedral is a painting of Tutul Xiu, *cacique*,[37] Maya tribal leader of the town of Mani, paying his respects to Francisco de Montejo at T'ho.[38] It was Tutul Xiu, the indigenous chief who had asked Montejo to help him defeat his Mayan enemy the Cocomes. The collaboration with Montejo was successful. The Cocomes were defeated, and too late, Tutul Xiu realized that the real enemy of the Maya was the Spanish Conquerors. With the defeat of the Cocomes, Xiu sealed the fate for the complete defeat of the Maya peoples. The painter of this scene had a definite Spanish conqueror perspective of local history. It is a sad reminder of the complete capitulation of the defeated Maya.

Next to the cathedral is the former archbishop's palace which houses the *Museo de Arte Contemporaneo*, now exhibiting the work of Yukatan's most noted contemporary painters and sculptures.

On the south side of the plaza is the *Casa de Montejo* dating from 1549. It served the Montejo family for almost 400 years. Into the stone façade of the building is carved a mural which shows the victorious abusing power over the native people by placing their feet on the necks of the vanquished. It feels creepy to be staring up at this carving. A few doors down from *Casa* is the entrance to my Hostel Zocalo, which isn't creepy at all.

On the west side of the plaza is the *Palacio Municipal* built in 1542. The Palacio was refurbished in 1730 and again in 1850. It serves, as it did earlier, as the city hall. It has a modern interior that is the location for dance and theater performances. It is on the same side of the street

---

37 *Cacique* is the Spanish word for tyrant, political boss, or chief. The Mayan translation from the Spanish is *batab, baatab, jalach, wiinik, tatich*.

38 T'ho is the name of the Mayan city which the Spanish Conquerors changed to their colonial capital, Merida.

where I sat that first evening for the free music concert.

On the north side of the plaza is the *Palacio de Gobierno* which houses Yucatán's executive state government and the tourist information center. It was built in 1892 as the site of the Palace of the Colonial Governors when this area was a colony of Spain before Mexican independence. Whether Spanish or Mexican, the *Palacio de Gobeirno* is the house of government. Inside the Palacio, on the walls of the first and second floor, are murals by local artist Fernando Castro Pacheco. Pacheco took twenty-five years to complete these murals portraying the history of the relationship between the Maya and the Spaniards. From the perspective of the Maya, I could feel the domination of the Colonial Spanish. The intense stories in these murals conveyed the hardships of the slaves

as they toiled in the fields, in the factories, and on hemp plantations. I found the paintings a powerful portrayal of the life of the conquered. They reminded me of the political turmoil in Diego Rivera's murals of the working people, paintings which have appeared in Mexico City, New York and Los Angeles. I wanted to linger and study these walls in more depth, but the guided tour was over; I was expected to leave.

The *Museo Regional de Antropologia*[39] is 10 blocks north of Grand Plaza. I

Nobility with facial serpent tattoo

---

39 The Regional Museum of Anthropology

Frieze of two jaguars, *Museo Regional de Antropologia*

head in that direction and visit banks along the way checking the exchange rate. Each was different than the one before; there was 12.22 pesos to the US dollar; next, 12.06; 12.10, and 12.40. I traded at the last bank, BancMultiva, across the street from the museum.

The Museum of Anthropology is housed in a pretentious mansion constructed by General Francisco Canton Rosado who lived in this home for only six years before his death. I swing open the tall wrought iron gate, climb the steps, and open the large carved wooden door to the lobby. At the admissions desk, my international teacher card is again declined, and I pay the full entrance fee of about six dollars and hire a guide for around twenty dollars. The guide is well prepared and the solo tour absorbs me totally. At the conclusion, I ask for a chair to sit and sketch. The staff tells me there is none, but I manage to hijack the lone white, plastic, portable picnic chair I saw in the corner of the first room I toured. It was in use then by a sleeping guard, but since the chair is now empty, I considered it up for grabs. I positioned myself across from the frieze of two jaguars, take out my pen and sketch pad and begin. This frieze reminded me of the panel on the temple I had seen at Chich'en two days ago. The jaguar was an important and powerful god of

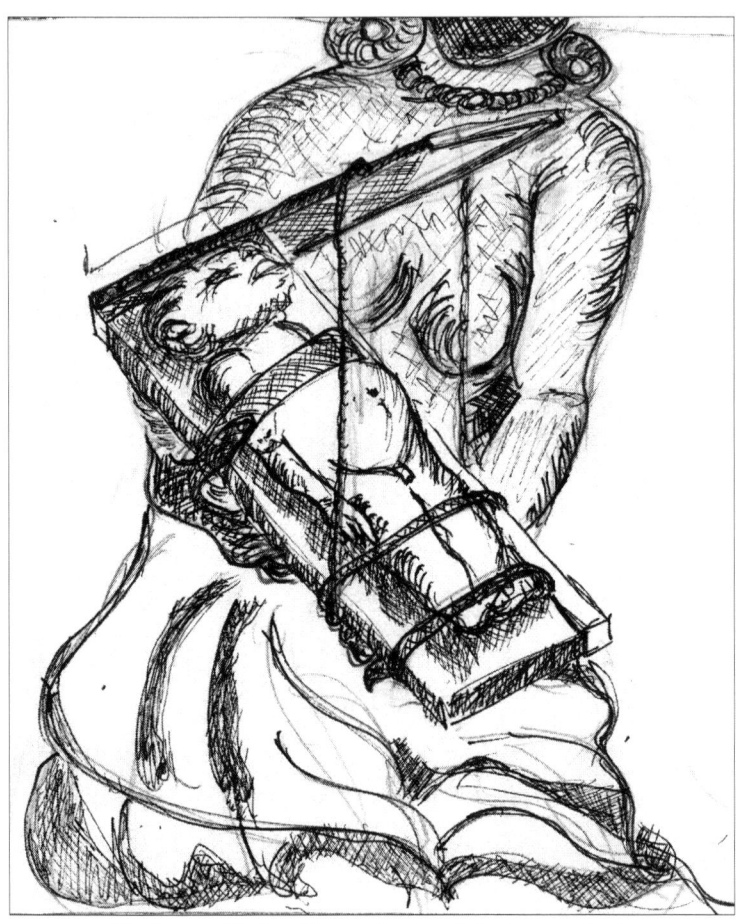

Mother and baby, *Museo Regional de Antropologia*

the Maya whose temple I had visited at Chich'en. This particular frieze might have fallen from such a temple. When my sketch was finished, I moved my chair to the next room.

This sketch is a diorama showing a Mayan mother holding her newborn baby strapped onto a wooden head board that places pressure against the newborn's forehead. So similar was this to the same baby head board design that I had seen in the Lewis and Clark museum on the Columbia River, that I wanted to study the similarities. Could there have been a cultural connection between these tribes? The practice of cranial deformation was the same.

It was almost five o'clock when the lady guard came to tell me the museum was closing. I quickly sketched, from a neighboring diorama, a few lines of a Mayan priest which I would complete later. I returned the plastic chair to the same corner for the next sleeping guard and left the museum.

The rain is returned. Pulling my rain shell around me, I walk back to Grande Plaza, stopping at a Kodak store and a grocery to pick up a disk and something for dinner. A young couple from Colorado on their honeymoon joined me at the common table in the kitchen of the hostel, and we dissected our day's adventures. Soon, I retreated to my room feeling it was a very good day in spite of the off and on rain. It didn't dampen my enthusiasm. Tomorrow, I would find my way to Uxmal.

Nobility only, sharpened teeth with imbedded jewels

Governor's House, Uxmal

El Palomar, Uxmal.

K'iin ●●●

5:33 A.M. Awakening to the sound of the humming paddle fan and the "good morning" song birds. I begin the routine: acclimate to morning air; take medicines with bottled water; take towel to bathroom. Returning from the communal bathroom, I look out the open courtyard to San Francisco Cathedral across the plaza. The lights in the steeple shine as bright beacons against the dusky new morning sky. According to the ancient beliefs of the Maya, the night has been defeated; the Gods of *Xibalbao*, the Gods of death, have lost. The new day, the creation, the re-birth has been victorious.

John of Mayan Riviera said that it was customary to wear white when visiting ancient sacred places, so I dress in the white loose-fitting Mayan dress from the Isle market. Although I am going early in the morning, the weather at Uxmal will be unbearably hot. Lightly, I pack writing materials, sketch book, money for bus fare and a little extra cash.

6:40 A.M. I emerge from my room ready for the day and watch the table being spread with freshly cut papaya, mango, pineapple, bananas, cereal, and yogurt. Oscar sees me eyeing the beautiful fruit and asks if I would like toast which he prepares on an over-the-stove flame grill. Moses, the owner, places a small plate of brie and salami on the table in front of me. A carton of eggs and bacon are set out for those guests who wish to cook their own, allowing two eggs per guest per day. When finished, guests wash their own dishes and leave them drying in the rack. Oscar cut the watermelon in wheel-like wedges. The papaya looked like petals of a golden colored flower. This breakfast was a visual treat and all included in my nightly fee of twenty dollars. It was the finest meal of my day and was by far superior to the two slices of toast, single banana and coffee, which was the breakfast routine at the Poc'na on Isla. I filled my water bottles from the tank at no extra charge (unlike the 10 pesos/bottle at Poc'na), headed down the marble steps, and out to the street.

Esquida quarto quadros. Esquida. Quarto quadros mais ate o terminal de autobus. Paga de autobus para Uxmal. (Left four blocks. Left. Four blocks more until the bus terminal. Take the bus for Uxmal.) After three long blocks, I turn left thinking I had gone far enough. Then I walked five or more blocks and was lost. I ducked into a *Hospital Maternidad* (Maternity Hospital) to ask directions. The long lines of women of all ages waiting to be seen told me there was no chance I was going to ask a question of staff, and that this facility was way overburdened with immediate need.

I walked another five minutes in the direction that I had originally been told and stopped at an intersection, asking the gentleman beside me. He pointed to the building behind the trees across the street from where we stood—The sign read, *"Terminal de Autobus—Mayba, Orient, ATS, and ADO."* The clock on the bus terminal wall reads 7:58. Purchasing a ticket for 46 pesos (about $4), I climb aboard and take the first two seats. There is ample room. I stretch my legs. Buckling my seat belt and placing my pack into the seat by the window, I take a deep breath and relax for the one and one-half hour ride to the holy Uxmal ruins, forty miles south of Merida.

9:30A.M. I pay my entrance fee of 116 pesos ($11) at the modern Unidad Uxmal building which houses an air conditioned restaurant; bathrooms with marbled sinks and beautiful tiles; lovely gift shops, and an educational display of anthropology discoveries. A young couple is entering at the same time I am and since we were the first visitors to the park this morning, I use the couple to show perspective in my photos. Although there are guides waiting to be hired, the government has set their fee at 500 pesos ($50) which is expensive for me as a solo guest. Unable to barter a government set fee, the guide book will have to do. With only the young couple ahead of me, I am on my own and glad to be ahead of the tour buses.

Like Chich'en, Uxmal was an important holy center. It was construct-ed on a dry plain and not near known *cenotes*.[40] Therefore, a series of *chultunes*[41] or cisterns bring deep ground water to the city. Collecting basins were also important. Posted signs asked us to be sensitive to wild-life. This might have referred to the lizards that lived among the rocks. I almost stepped on one which had adapted to a rock color camouflage.

The *Casa Del Adivino*, or Magician's House as the name translates, is the first building at the top of the entrance ramp. It is oval shaped with rounded corners. The structure has been rebuilt five times, one temple on top of the other in Chenes style. The main doorway was the mouth of a *Chaac* mask. Directly behind this structure is the *Quadrangulo de las Monjas* or Nuns'quadrangle, so named because of its 74-room complex. Archeologists speculate on the function of this building as a possible military academy, royal school, or palace complex. Four temples make up the quadrangle. The face and nose of the Rain God *Chaac* are designed into each temple, and *Kulkulcan*, the plumed or feathered serpent is also prominent in the building façade. I walk through the *Juego de Pelota* or Ball Court and climb up very steep paved steps to the higher platform to stand next to the *Casa de Las Tortugas*, House of the Turtles so named because of the row of turtle figures that are seen at intervals atop vertical, carved column stones that circle the building. The lower part of the façade is unadorned and is considered a Classic Puuc style. Next to Rain God *Chaac*, the turtles were thought to bring the rains to this dry area.

Beyond the corbelled arch of the *El Palomar*[42] are façade rocks long dislodged from their original placement like strewn pieces of a giant

---

40 The *cenotes* (pronounced "she-noh-tays") and derived from the Maya word *d'zonot*, meaning "water-filled cavern" are limestone sink holes which traditionally served as watering holes, fresh water natural cisterns. The caves "are formed by the erosive effects of rainwater drilling down through the porous limestone" (Lonely Planet). Unique to the Yucatan, there are an estimated 3000 cenotes which modern visitors use for swimming and snorkeling. People of the Yucatan are dependent upon the underground water system.

41 The *chultunes* or cisterns were constructed into the buildings

42 *El Palomar* is the dovecot, a shelter for doves or pigeons. *Paloma* in Spanish is dove, pigeon.

puzzle, or so I thought until two of the pieces moved, and I recognized iguanas creeping away from me. I stopped. They stopped. We studied each other. Counting nine pairs of eyes upon me and respecting *their* habitat, I slowly back up, go around the pile of stones on the far side, and leave them in peace.

Disturbing the lizard rock pile was entirely my fault because I was off the beaten tourist path, searching for the *Casa de la Vieja* (Old Woman's House). My guide book explained that in front of this structure was a small *palapa* (thatched-roof hut) protecting several large stone phalluses. I was interested in the connection between the old woman's house and the phalluses, but it was not as the guide book described. I found only a raised platform of a two-headed jaguar seat, which itself was a place of leadership and power for whomever sat upon it. In the center of the field, behind the jaguar seat, was only one very large carved phallus stone structure. The guide book did not explain the disappearance of the other phalluses, information more easily obtained from the paid tour guides.

Before returning to town, there was time to peruse the gift shops, study the arts, crafts, educational exhibits, and have a relaxing lunch in the air-conditioned restaurant. At 2:00 o'clock, tour guides were gone for the day and the only people present were tired tourists waiting for the bus.

Wooden lintel doorway, Uxmal.

I boarded the same bus with the same driver as this morning and carrying an extra parcel—a lightweight, bulky black gourd on which three Mayan glyphs were etched. I may research in Michael Coe's, *Breaking the Maya Code* to decipher the meaning of the glyphs. Meanwhile, I appreciate the art, and it will add take up space in my backpack. Across the bus aisle were two familiar looking ladies. The older says in local Spanish which I translate here to Portuguese, *"Voce fui a la museo de antropologia ontem."*[43]

"Sim." I really wanted to add, but held my tongue, a*nd you were the guard who asked me to leave.* The younger woman had taken my admissions fee. Both treated me with kindness and seemed pleased to see me on this trip. A familiar man and his son, who had also taken the morning bus, boarded. They greeted me as well. During the ride back to Merida, I fell asleep to the rhythm of the tires on pavement. When we arrived back at the bus terminal, the man and his son offered to help me with directions toward Grande Plaza and Hostel Zocalo. We walked together, and I appreciated the company.

That evening, checking my e-mails, I let the family and friends know I am safe, hot, and starting to miss home. Weather reports of a tropical depression were causing some worry back in Olympia. Art friend Ed e-mailed me, *"Keep journaling."* Remembering my journal, I retreat to the balcony. As musicians below tune their guitars for another summer evening of music and offer me their serenade; and as the sky turns from sky blue to royal navy above my head, I write.

Dyox botik[44]

Dios bo'otik[45]

Gracias[46]

---

43   *"You were at the anthropology museum yesterday."*
44   Pronounced "dee-osh bow teek" is Mayan for "thank you."
45   "Thank you" as published in *Diccionario Maya de bolsillo*.
46   "Thank you" in Spanish

Chaac, Uxmal

K'iin ●●●●

Papaya, melon, mango, grapefruit, banana, pineapple, cartons of yogurt, hot coffee, and cereal greet the hostel guests this morning. Lingering over the tasty fruit, I plan my day to the *cenotes*. Hostel day manager Oscar assures me this trip is well worth taking. I descend the marble staircase and follow his directions to *Parque de San Juan* where a *combi*, a small van, is filling with passengers. Only when the seats are full will the driver depart to Cuzuma, where I make connections to visit three *cenotes*.[47] A swimming suit and towel are tucked into my day pack. With the description in *Lonely Planet* and Oscar's enthusiastic support, "swimming in *cenote*" will be checked off the "to-do" list. This story is one for the swim team.

The packed *combi* is a two-hour ride for a fare of 17 pesos (about $1.50). We pass through small villages, discharging passengers and taking on others. When the *combi* pulls into the central plaza, several young men are waiting with their Pedi trikes and motor carts. These are either bicycles or small motorcycles with a seated platform in front of the peddler or driver, hand rails, and awning. A price is negotiated. I step onto the platform. Down a paved road we go for three miles. I feel exposed being out in front, but loaded trucks pass us easily and the skill of my driver reassures me. I relax and enjoy the ride feeling a bit like that of a kid being carried on bike handlebars.

As we turn off the road and enter into an empty gravel parking lot,

---

47 Sacred pools for ceremonial purposes; limestone sinkholes that can be viewed from holes in the land above; healing waters. There are thousands of these pools and underground fresh water streams on which the early populations depended. Without these watering holes, the people could not survive in this arid, jungle environment.

I am jolted from my reverie, the first guest to arrive. Horses with sisal harnesses wait in the shade. Handlers are waiting to hook them up as needed to wooden carts over steel wheels which placed by hand onto a small rail track which leads into the bush. The price for the estimated three-hour round trip will be 200 pesos (about $20). Although my guide book says 150 pesos for four people, there is only one of me, and the price seems in the ballpark of "okay." A manager assigns me to a team of two men who set about positioning the cart on the track and hitching the horse. Then, the two men sit on the front bench as if my cart were a grand stage coach and off we go into the dense, lush, bushy jungle of what used to be an old *henequen* or sisal hacienda. Half an hour later, we arrive at the first *cenote*.

A cabana up a hill complete with flush toilet, dressing room, and thatched roof has been constructed in the middle of the thicket. I change into my swim suit and come out with the white cotton Mayan dress as my cover-up. The horse/cart team is mine for the day, so I place my shoes, dress, eye glasses, and bag onto the cart and proceed to the top of the stairs that descend to the water surface. At the bottom of the double flight of wooden stairs, stone steps guide me to the water's edge. Within the deep, damp cave, I appreciate the wide sunny opening to the upper "ground" level. Sliding into the water is immediately refreshing, not too cold and not too hot either. The water is dark and deep. Sound of birds chattering as they enter and leave the cave is amplified, bouncing back from the walls to my ears. Not wearing glasses, my sense of hearing is amplified as well in the enclosure. Making a circuit of the circumference of this private cave pool, I examine the inside of the rocky walls. Turning over and floating on my back, I examine the cave ceiling, and gently flutter kick as to not disturb the calming effect of this place. After floating like this for what seems to be half an hour, I glide to the bottom steps, pull myself out of the water and walk up the wooden staircase. Other guests have now arrived.

My timing was perfect. I slip the white dress/cover-up over my suit, replace my sandals, and look for my glasses. They have disappeared.

Finally, after a rather frightening fifteen minutes of not having vision to find my glasses, the young driver locates them where they slid off the cart and into the bushes when the cart was moved to make room for an approaching cart. That is the system. There is one track for carts going to and from each *cenote*. The drivers must decide who stops and removes the cart from the track and who is allowed to go straight through. Sometimes, when meeting another cart, my drivers stop and motion for me to disembark. The horse is unhitched and the cart is removed from the track. When the other cart has passed through, my cart assumes the right-of-way and we begin again. Sometimes, it is my cart that can go straight through.

It is forty-five minutes before we reach the second cenote. As we walk toward the entrance platform, the driver shows me a small, perhaps one square foot wide, hole in the ground. Gazing into and below ground surface, this hole has immense depth and opens into a cave into which I will soon descend. Stepping back, I wonder if the ground will be strong enough to hold without sending me tumbling into the cave below. The platform displays a caution sign. Entrance to this *cenote* is a worn hand-built wooden ladder in which each step is

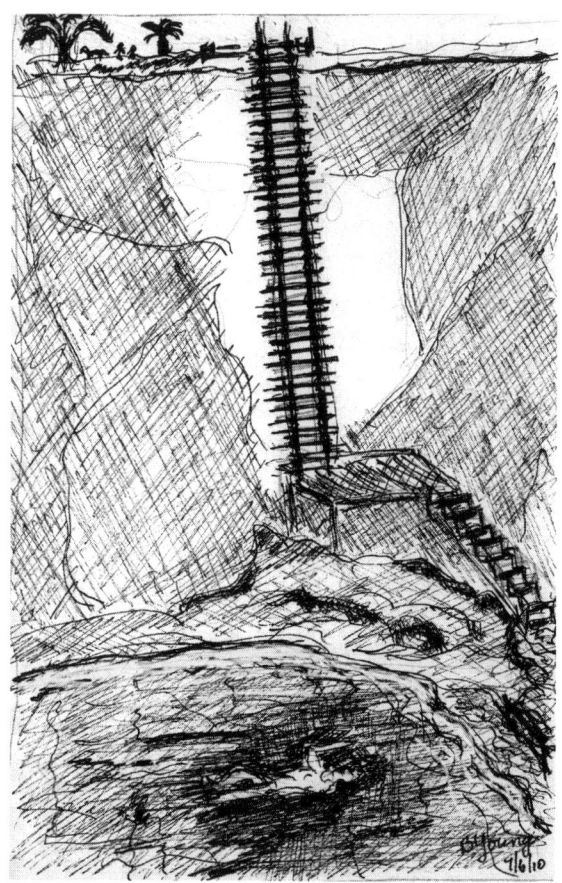

rope lashed to long poles, thirty rope steps straight down. Concentrating on one step at a time and testing to see that my feet are firmly placed before I move the next foot, I slowly descend. At the bottom of the ladder is a small wooden deck. Five more steps over rock lead to another latticed ladder that reaches below the water's surface. Scooting slowly, I move my body forward as it is dark and I am not yet acclimated, alone in the cave. In addition to the light from the ladder entrance, there is the small hole the driver showed me earlier, allowing a shaft of light to shine directly onto the pool, through the pool, and into the depths of the water. Long ropes of vine-y vegetation clinging to the rock ceiling surface reaches for water below. I swim in and out of these ropes without touching them, not wanting to dislodge them from the ground above.

After a while, a young couple descends the ladder. No longer private, I transition from my meditative solitude to a shared space and welcome them. From Slovakia, on their honeymoon. Considering that I have been here already long enough, I ask the young man to extend his hand so that I am better able to access the rung of the ladder within the surface of the pool. This challenging exit from water to rock ledge is not unlike the exit of the lake I experienced as a child in Ohio. The access ladder is directly under the end of the wooden dock and you must pull yourself straight up the slimy step and over the end of the dock. Having accomplished this, I scoot backwards up the stone steps and begin to climb carefully, one-at-a time, the thirty rope-step ladder, leaving the honeymooners to their own privacy in the pool.

Returning to above ground surface, I was struck by the day's intense heat. Seeing me approach, the drivers replaced the cart, hitched the horse, and we were back on track to the third and last *cenote*.

For the second time today, I descend a wide, wooden stairway with hand rail that feels safer and more secure than the lashed rope pole ladder. Again, I swim the circumference of the pool and enjoy the solitude, coolness, and quiet of another *cenote* cave space. I understood the importance of these sacred pools to the survival of a population who existed in such an arid land. Water deep below the surface was the reassurance that the community would survive.

After a thirty-minute cool down from the heat above, I was ready to climb out of my retreat and ascend the steps to the ground surface. Re-connecting with my driving team, the young horse, *cavalito*, picked up the pace to the parking lot. Waiting three hours since my entrance into the jungle, was the young pedi trike driver. He peddled me back to Cuzuma town plaza where a fifteen passenger van was filling for a return to Merida. We waited forty-five minutes to reach capacity. Feeling the heat and sitting in an already crowded van, I dozed. It was dinner time when we finally reached Merida.

———

The Grand Plaza was in a state of great preparation, traffic being diverted. A grandstand was being set up on the corner nearest my hostel, the *Casa de Montejo* side of the plaza. People were gleeful, wanting to celebrate. This very evening would be a community celebration for Merida's new mayor, a woman, who, it is believed, would end corruption of the previous mayor. Enthusiastic townspeople wanted improvements, an end to the skimming of riches by those in power, much like the class system of the ancient Maya. Noble class built elaborate temples to their Gods who gave them authority and power over the community. Farmers, from the bottom of the social system, fed the city. If the Rain God *Chaac* did not perform and bring the rains to grow the crops, who was at fault? Ancient rulers of *Chich'en Itza* were a council that met regularly within the Temple of Warriors. In modern Merida, a corrupt regime was being replaced by a female leader, an action unheard of in the ancient city. Thinking the second story balcony would be a very good place to take pictures, I slipped through the crowd to get my camera battery checked at the Kodak store, moving away from the grandstand to the opposite corner of the plaza where streets were still open for shopping.

———

The Sting. Passing a vendor selling nice-looking "Panama" hats and pausing long enough to hear his spiel. I bought a fedora-type. Proceeding on down the street and feeling a bit smug with my new hat, a student of the university caught up with me and asked if he might walk with me and practice his English. I was flattered since helping college students was my job and did not doubt he was other than what he told me. He asked if I wanted to see the art gallery at the Centro Cultural Universitario across the street. Yes. I responded to the offer. Art was on my "to see in Merida list" and this was my last evening to do so.

This building was the first university, my student guide explained, *built in the 17th century*. We walked into the building and art gallery. A plush, private event was being set up in the court yard, elegant preparations: white linens, crystal glasses, fine china and table service, and large colorful floral bouquets. A walk through the art gallery exposed faculty and student contemporary pieces.

Back on the street again, the student asked if I wanted to see some of the local arts and crafts made by village artisans and sold through the cooperative. *Yes.* The cooperative was on my list, too. Around the corner was a cooperative where the student introduced me to a nice looking salesman. The student then excused himself and said he needed to go back to work. My attention became riveted to the salesman's colorful stories of local artisans: the weaving and knotting of the *henequen* hammocks, the quality of the panama hats made in the villages surrounding Merida, and when I asked about the reboza observed on the shoulders of merchant women, the salesman sent a messenger to another store to obtain exactly what was described. With the help of my VISA card, I purchased one hammock, one new large brimmed hat, and one reboza that matched those of the merchant women. Walking back to the hostel and mulling over the three very pricey purchases, I reviewed the evening's interactions with the hat vendor, student who wanted to speak English, and the salesman with stories.

When the music started, I was on the balcony, feeling the amplified vibrations of a ramped-up sound system, which all too soon bounced me back inside to the solitude of my room. During the night, I awoke several times to perseverate those three purchases: a hammock which probably was not made of mosquito repealing henequen and for which I have no hammock stand or trees from which to suspend it; the wide-brimmed panama hat of which I now have two; and the *reboza* of silk threads which probably is of rayon. I had the sinking feeling that I had been taken in—the gullible social "do-gooder" person wanting to support a social cooperative. The bait: interesting storytelling of rural craftsmanship and crafty salesmanship. Deciding that the next day all three purchases would be returned to the cooperative, I finally fell asleep. It seemed like a resolution that would prevent excessive vacation expense, reduce the weight of my backpack, and save my Scottish pride.

K'iin ▃▃▃

As Hostel Zocala owner Moses was pampering us at breakfast with extra brie and salami in addition to the usual array of fine fruits, I asked to discuss my cooperative store experience. Moses speaks only Spanish and as I explained the story, he pulled Oscar into the discussion. They both encouraged me to try to negotiate with the cooperative. As back-up support, I could involve the Office of Turismo. The office could also call in the municipal police. My goal is to return the three items and get credit for the total. It was my absorption into good storytelling, but paying many times the value of the item is not how I want to support the cooperative.

I stop at the Office of Turismo and explain my plan. They, too, en-courage me to negotiate. They are all young people, perhaps new to their jobs, and would prefer this conflict did not exist. I tell them I will report the outcome of my negotiation. I leave their office feeling that it is entirely up to me to resolve my issue. Arriving at the store a few minutes before nine o'clock, I find women arranging the merchandise. They tell me the man with whom I need to speak will reach the store at 9:30 to 10:00. In the next half-hour, I shop other stores to check the prices of hammocks, panama hats, and rebozas. Gathering information and returning promptly at 9:30, another employee telephones the man, and he promises to arrive at ten-thirty. I pull up a chair and watch the soccer game: Holland vs. Brazil. Holland won two goals to one. It is 10:50 and the man has not appeared. I continue to wait. Another man appears and says he may be able to help me since the man for whom I am waiting will not come until the next day. He wants to know what the problem is. I tell him I have been to the Office of Tourismo and can ask the Police Municipal for assistance. I want to negotiate in good faith and return all items for which I was charged 10 times the value, for a credit of 6,000 pesos (somewhat less than $US 600 dollars). The man entered a credit, 60 pesos (about $US 4.64). I pointed to his error with the zeros. He must submit again. He said he could only enter one time. I said enter one time again. Then, one time enter again. Then enter a third time for the complete return. He said he couldn't do that. We went back and forth until noon. I tried not to feel beaten and needed to be strong to stay in the game, aware, too, when the afternoon bus was scheduled to leave for Cancun. It was Friday, business would slack off, and nothing would be negotiated over the week-end. I was feeling "touristy" and disappointed and wanted to leave town. He probably wanted me to leave, too, without my full credit and with the offending purchases. Remembering the words of the Office de Tourismo staff, obtaining partial credit, I asked the man to enter another credit. He entered a credit of $M 3,000 pesos, one-half of the original receipt. I caved in and signed for it. That was half of the charge. I picked up a boiled wool tote that I could carry my sketch book in and signed the credit. Calculate any loss of this whole deal would be made up in the satisfaction of telling the story. I turned and walked out of the cooperative, stopping by the Tourist Office to report a lesson learned.

At the same Tourist Office, I purchase my bus ticket, paying $M268 for a first class ticket, Merida to Cancun on the ADO. Second class Orient would have been $M114. ADO was express and leaving the station at 2:30. I was ready to be pampered, take the service offered and leave town. I did not want to negotiate.

Having lunch on the plaza at the open air café, a hammock maker approached me and said that he made the hammocks in his own home. I believed him. His hammock looked just like the one I purchased in the store. His price was less than $US20. Later, back in Olympia, I visited Dick Meyer at the Traditions Fair Trade store. Dick complimented me on the panama hat I was wearing, selling a similar looking hat for $25.00. The *reboza* remains a mystery as I have not seen the same scarf again. I believe that the lesson for me to learn is to enjoy the stories, honor those who spend the hours making these beautiful things, laugh at my errors in judgment, and appreciate that the salesman assessed me better than I assessed myself. I'll need to find a hammock stand and invite friends over to try it out. I will wear my panama hat to protect from the sun. I will wear the reboza as proudly as the women I saw in Merida. Thank you for the lessons. *Dyox bo tik.*

When my VISA statement came, and I could estimate the international exchange between pesos and dollars, this was the fallout of my three purchases: $M6,000 was $US464.02 for the hammock, panama hat, and *reboza*. I was first credited for $US4.59 and .13 for foreign tax refund. I was also credited US$232.01 and foreign tax fee refund of US$6.96.

In U.S. dollars: originally charged:	464.02
Credits by cooperative and federal tax:	4.59
	.13
	232.01
	6.96
	243.69
Originally charged:	464.02
Credits subtracted:	-243.69
Total cost to me:	220.33

Compare the $220.33 with what I might have purchased in Olympia at Traditions: Hammock ($20); hat ($25); reboza (estimate $50), for a total of under $100.00 and without the hustling and hassle. Hoping that the profits go back to the craftspeople and weavers of hammocks, hats, and *rebozos* in small rural villages of the Yucatán, I relinquish my story.

———

The bus ride from Merida to Cancun was comfortable with air conditioning and movies. I composed a poem about my cenotes visit and kept laying the poem aside to see more of the movie dubbed in Spanish. Meryl Streep and her girl friends were cavorting in a Greek Villa in *MamaMia*. The second feature showed actor Will Smith was in a drama where he let a sting ray get him in an icy bathtub. I should have stayed with the poem writing. Four hours later, we arrive at the bus terminal in Cancun. Avoiding the long line of travelers to hail a taxi for $M50, I walk to the far side of the building and hail a cab for $M20 to Porto Juarez.

At the ferry terminal, I opted for the bright yellow tourist boat. Standing in line beside tourists laden with bags, I boarded with back pack, stowing it with all other baggage, freeing me to move about the boat. I chose to ride on the hard benches of the upper, open-air level with four other passengers. The majority stayed below in blue, plush, reclining seating well protected behind glass windows from the splash of the sea. The horizon over the sea was settling into a glorious golden orange sunset. Feeling a salty, misty breeze on my cheeks as the boat picks up speed, I take a deep breath and relax. We were returning to *Isla*.

————

Back at Poc'na Hostel, I requested a private room. The receptionist guided me to the tower: across the court yard, past the blooming red hibiscus, to the very back of the building, climbing two flights to the third floor. The narrow, steep steps reminded me of *El Castillo*. She unlocked the door to a beautiful room with full sized bed, a sliding glass door that opened to a full view of the sea and three windows that faced the street on the east. There was a writing desk, extra chair, book case and bench. I sit down on the bench to unhook my pack's waist band, let it ease into the wall, and slip my arms from the shoulder straps. I arrange sketch book and writing materials on the desk, switch on the paddle fan, and feel at home. I return to the common room for news.

Nancy, my former women's dorm mate introduces me to Ruth, a special education teacher from Bellevue, Washington, who was also a Returned Peace Corps Volunteer. We made plans to meet the next day. I returned to the tower where I picked up *The Popol Vuh in the Mayan*

Art, a reference book purchased Merida bookstore. I wanted to understand the creation of the Maya people, according to the legends and as
interpreted from their sacred recordings. It was calming and comfortable to be back on the island.

Waiting for tourists, Port, Isle Mujeres

K'iin ==●==

Looking out at the eternal movement of the water on predetermined
time schedules, I listen to the roar of the waves coming ashore, dis-
sipating, and returning to the sea. I think of People who have lived
classic periods, and then their culture declines to allow another People
to come forward to take leadership and occupy the place of the former.
I consider our political system and wonder if our leaders will take our
country forward with innovation or allow our civilization to decline,
to be taken over by the next world leader. The ancient Maya ruled by
council and put their faith into Gods that explained their existence,
their reason for being, their re-creation and death and their constant
change in re-creation and rebirth. The Maya lived with a balance of the
months in accordance with study of the heavens, the moon, the sun
and the seasons.

Breaking from musing on the meaning of life and the decline of
cultures and needing people contact, I head downstairs for the usual
breakfast of toast, banana, and coffee. As I sit at a long table, a tall,
attractive, young Anglo woman sits close to me, opens her laptop and
talks rather loudly into her Skype connection in a language unfamiliar.
When she has completed her conversation, she closes up her computer
and moves away, never acknowledging my presence. It goes like this at
times, and it makes me feel a bit dated or aged, that I have nothing to
share with these healthy, young, international travelers. I do have these
hang-ups: I think that a private conversation is conducted in private. A
greeting or acknowledgement of existence by someone who sits down
next to you is appropriate. Yet, I did not greet the young woman.

As I reflect on my own behavior in that situation, a composed and confident woman approaches. She asks if she might sit down. "Yes, of course." She is familiar to me, but I cannot remember the connection and tell her so.

She replies, "When we met, you were washing your clothes in the hostel restroom in Merida, are from near Seattle and teach psychiatric nursing. I am a teacher, too. Did you go to Tulum?

Memory surged. "Of course, you are the international instructor who has traveled around the world. I scrapped Tulum from my visit list, preferring to return to Isle before my flight to the states."

Smiling, "I'm Valerie. You tend to meet the same people when you backpack as we do."

The pleasant repartee made up for the lack of communication earlier and reaffirmed that you do meet interesting people.

Back in my tower, I study the vivid blue-green of the water which seems to be emphasized by the color of sky changing from pale blue to light grey to deeper blue-grey. A storm is coming. The gray sky highlights the six damaged palm trees on the boardwalk. They shudder as if in remembrance of the hurricane that hit Cancun a few years ago. As it is so with other creatures in this changing environment, these palms struggle to survive.

I close the windows to the alley against the rain now coming onto

my writing table, and wait it out as storms here usually don't last long, expecting that the sky to soon turn from dark to light again.

Sounds from the common room waft up from the inner courtyard to the tower, a strong rendition of the Argentine National Anthem. Germany vs. Argentina. Soccer finals are close. A few of the guests are from Germany and wonder if we'll hear their anthem as well. I descend from my quiet loft to the action below. On the big TV screen, international soccer players from many teams unroll a huge banner which reads, *Support no racism*. After a brief display, the banner is rolled up again, and the games begin.

Rain has come and gone. The sun is shining, warming the injured palms and returning visitors to the beach. Couples watch the waves, others take pictures. A few park their motorized carts and move closer to the water. Back in my room, I re-open the windows before leaving the tower for the streets. As I pass again through the common room, the soccer crowd has gone and a few remaining guests are now watching *Big Fish*, a Spanish dubbed movie starring Albert Finney. I continue on my way.

K'iin ☴

July 4, 2010! Happy Birthday to daughter Katherine on her thirty-eighth birthday! The Poc'na has the benefit of free computer use for a half hour. Sitting my turn on a small hard bench in the tiny computer room, I am third in the queue. This is national Election Day and there was no drinking allowed anywhere on the island last evening or today. I learned that this "no drinking when votes are cast" rule holds the voters accountable for free-from-vote buying with alcohol-free elections, a ruling fairly well enforced even though it may have cut into profits of the resort restaurants.

I have been in my sea-view room for two nights and have enjoyed the solitude but have made the decision to move to another hostel later in the day, one that Ruth discovered closer to the center of town for 100 pesos (about $10) per night. My private, sea-view, third floor, walk-up will be exchanged for a room with private shower, less expensive, and less human traffic with backpacks and laptop computers. Another advantage is that Ruth leaves Mexico for Washington State the same time and day as I do, and we can share rides off the island, into Cancun, and to the airport. We stay at a quiet family hostel which is not listed in *Lonely Planet* but well might be. There is time now to check out the various dive shops to see if this one item on my "to do" list might yet be accomplished.

Visiting Crystal Dive Shop on the main drag, Carey Dive Shop which is closed, and the Sea Hawk Dive Shop, I check fees, description of the dives and qualifications of the dive companies. By nine in the morning, instructors and guides have already left, talking clients to scheduled dives. Valerie told me yesterday that she is a diver and prefers Honduras where the prices are less expensive and the locations are every bit as beautiful. It seems prudent for me to postpone a deep sea dive. It has been twenty years since I passed my PADI certification, and it would be safer to take a refresher course.

Passing through the court yard on my return to Poc'na, I stop to appreciate a very large, red, hibiscus bush. Pulling a white plastic deck chair close, I sketch.

Tucking away my sketch materials, I climb the steps to my tower room and begin the transition of hostel living, packing backpack with lightest items at the bottom and heavier items toward the center, distributing weight for less strain on the back. The pack expands to accommodate my purchases, but with the extra bulk, I had to think myself thin to navigate down the narrow, twisty steps. I say good-bye to my tower perch and head down the cobbled street.

Ruth has returned from a day with the whale sharks, the biggest fish in the ocean, and is bubbling with enthusiasm; yet, complaining of being dizzy and a bit nauseated. Nancy thinks it is dehydration from a day in the sun on the water and insists we all walk to the grocery store to buy a hydration supplement of coconut water. Convinced that Ruth's experience with the whale sharks would make an inspiring last day in the Yucatán, I dip into reserve cash and determine there is enough to pay for the adventure.

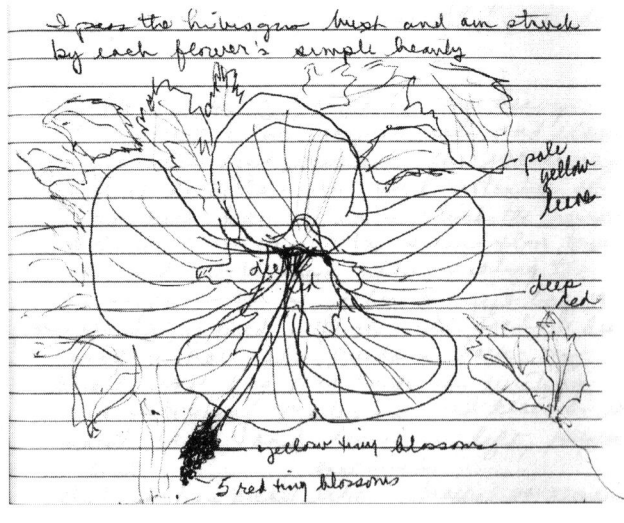

K'iin ●●●

Standing with the "Swim with the Whale Sharks" salesman at the Isla Mujeres dock, I wait for the dive boat to collect me before it continues on its way to the Cancun mainland side of the bay. The sail across the water gives me one-on-one time with dive instructor Arturo to learn the intricacies of his work in teaching tourists to swim with big fish who have come to this area to feed. Across the water, we pick up the other hopeful swimmers and receive our instructions as to rules of the swim:

1. We are not permitted to touch the sea animals.

2. We are to swim strongly alongside the whale shark.

3. We are to keep splashing to a bare minimum as we enter the water.

4. We are to respect the fish during this time of feeding.

5. We swim in pairs led by the dive instructor.

6. We do not talk, and we are to follow the dive instructor's hand signals.

We must keep our heads in the water to observe the position of the fish below the surface.

If another dive boat is in the same area, the swimmers will enter the water only on the instructor's order, and no more than two swimmers and an instructor are allowed beside the whale shark.

We are to follow the rules, respect the animals, instructor, partner, and the sea.

All swimmers are given a plastic name band as if we were signing into the hospital for care and place our signatures on the official documents not holding the company responsible if we are lost at sea. I purchase an underwater camera with my last U.S. dollars, hoping to prove to my grandchildren that this is more than a virtual swim. Swimmers wear life jackets, snorkel mask, breathing tube, and fins.

Boarding again, we leave for an hour's ride, somewhere to the north. Our destination is the area where the currents of the Caribbean Sea flow into meet the Gulf of Mexico. Currently in their feeding cycle, whale sharks are mouth eaters and swim against the current allowing the plankton caught in the current to flow through their teeth into their mouths. The captain finds the fish where the currents are the strongest. I sit under the canopy for shade, wear a T-shirt over my suit, and generously lather arms and legs with sunscreen. When the captain arrives at the animals' feeding area, we see other dive boats, discharging their swimmers. Arturo gives us the order in which we, in assigned pairs, enter the sea. I swim last with Arturo. We get three jumps.

Swimmers are instructed to sit on the gunnels of the boat and swing one leg over the edge. When the captain sights the "partner" whale shark, he slowly glides the boat as close to the animal as he can, leaving a small area for the swimmer to jump. When the dive instructor determines the time is right, he yells, "Jump!" The pair slides into the water, find the whale shark, and swim at its side against the current. This lasts but a few minutes, then the swimmers find their way back to the port side of the boat, grab the ladder and pull themselves back into the hold. Each pair of swimmers goes through this exercise with varying levels of success. Finally, it is my turn and I position myself on the gunwale.

"Jump! and I am in the sea. Fumbling with the snorkel, and fighting the breathing pattern, I forget to hold my head in the water as instructed or to breathe through the tube, trying instead to use my conditioned breathing pattern of the U.S. Masters swim group at the "Y". I am exhausted struggling to understand, I did not even see the fish, swim to the port side of the boat, lift my fins to be taken aboard, and pull myself up the ladder. Safely back on the bench, I practice using the snorkel tube for in and out exchange of air, leaving the mouthpiece in place. I visualize my head under the surface, using the snorkel tube to breath.

For my second jump, I am partnered with Byron, a tall, handsome young father, a policeman from Colorado. "Jump!" I see the whale shark, keep my head down, and position myself for the swim. Byron swims between me and the fish. My concentration is disrupted as Byron swims too close to the animal, panics, and touches the animal to distance himself from it. The whale shark dives away from us and we return to the boat. I was able to breathe and keep my head in the water. For my third and last jump, I again have Arturo as my partner and guide. He takes my underwater camera and agrees to take pictures; I agree to keep my head down, breathe through the snorkel tube, and swim alongside the whale shark.

"Jump!" Responding to Arturo's hand signal, I put my head down, breathe through the snorkel tube, repeating to myself, *keep your head down. Breathe.* Using fins, I intensify the power of the flutter kick, and I hear the shouts of my hometown swim Coach Laurel yelling, *Kick! Kick! Kick!* My head is under the surface, and I keep it there as to not lose this experience. I swim beside the animal, incredibly beautiful, graceful, many times my size and weight, noticing the large gills opening and closing on the side of her body. I mimic her confidence. I am a guest in her world, wanting to show respect, fully aware of the honor she has given me to allow this brief intimate partnership. We swim as partners against the current.

Too soon my energy is spent. I lift my head out of the water and see Arturo surface as well. He gives me a "thumbs up." I turn over on my back, feel the buoyancy of a super thick life jacket, and with my arms and legs extended and relaxed, allow the waves to rock me back and forth. Looking to the sky, I offer a prayer of thanksgiving for the life of the animal. Quite pleased, swimming to port side and holding my finned feet up for help in removing, I climb the ladder and pull myself aboard. I replace all the equipment; drink water, snack on fruit, and move to a shady seat under the canopy. I am satisfied and doze as the captain turns the boat homeward for our sail back to port.

―――

The host at the family hostel brings me aloe vera for my red sunburned knees. Then, I walk with Ruth to the grocery store to purchase coconut water. Leaving the hostel, we are looking for a nice fish restaurant for our last dinner and are immediately distracted and buy bread pudding from the lady selling it out of her car at the end of the street. Walking several more blocks finds us on the plaza where we are attracted to the taco vendor, choosing chicken, pork, or beef. Another vendor sells crème Brule in small paper cups. Choosing an empty bench facing the plaza in front of the municipal building, we savor our choices. Returning to our hostel, we pass tables set with candlelight at restaurants to which the guests are arriving. The attitude is relaxed, pleasant, loving, and friendly, and we soak up the ambiance, knowing that in the morning, we are on the first ferry to leave the island, sailing to the mainland, busing to the airport, and returning to our homes and lives in the Pacific Northwest.

Swimming with a whale shark

K'inn ●●●●

Waking before Ruth's alarm, I shower, apply the last of my sun block to sore knees, pack the last items into the backpack, arrange the decorative gourd from Uxmul into the cloth tote from the Riviera promotional, and strip the bed. When the room is clean, we slip into our backpacks, gather sheets, towels, room keys, and turn these in to our hostel host. It is raining; we pull on rain jackets. Our thank you's conveyed and good-byes said, we depart for the ferry. Once aboard, the sailing is rough, and hearing of storms coming, we're glad to be heading away from the island.

Arriving at Porto Juarez, the streets were already filled with water as the rain is unrelenting. An elevated crosswalk, rather like a high speed bump in an American street, allows us to cross without wading. Knowing we were about to board the bus, a taxi driver shouted he could help, charging 30 pesos to the bus terminal. Considering quickly: the fare is usually 20 pesos; taxi drivers closer to the entrance of the ferry were asking 50; there were two of us and our backpacks...

Sim,[48] was my quick response and he hoisted our packs into the trunk. Climbing into the back seat, we were out of the rain. The driver bartered to take us directly to the airport for 250 pesos ($25). We repeated two more times that we were going to the bus terminal for 30 pesos ($3). "*Vamos ao terminal de autobus por trinta pesos.*"[49]

At 7:47 A.M., we arrive at the bus terminal and purchase tickets on the first class bus for 42 pesos (about $4). At 8:30, we depart and by 9:00 we arrive at the international airport. Ruth heads to Delta; I, to AirTran, both leaving the Yucatán peninsula for the Seattle. There is no queue at

---

48 Portuguese for "yes."
49 We go to the bus terminal for thirty pesos.

the front desk and am quickly processed through security. The woman in front of me is wearing a lovely Mayan inspired embroidered blouse; her husband is reading a paper-back copy of *Three Cups of Tea*. My pack is not as light today as it was when I traveled across the pampas in Argentina some forty-two years ago, heading home from Peace Corps service, but it really isn't heavy now either. When the Maya left their homes and abandoned their community, what did they take with them?

Did they use a backpack?

It is late in the evening when the plane touches down in Seattle. With full backpack, cloth tote from the Mayan Riviera, boiled wool bag from the Merida cooperative, I arrive with memories of pleasant travel and gentle people. I also have a very large fish story and lessons of creation, rebirth, life and death of an ancient civilization. I am transformed from day-to-day budget conscious travel to one moved by the lessons of both the ancient and the modern Mayan people. I am touched spiritually by a whale shark who allowed me to swim as a partner in a beautiful underwater realm not my own.

My sister and brother-in-law pick me up at the baggage area and we head south on Interstate 5 toward Olympia and home. After a good night's rest, the new day will defeat the darkness and I will be reborn. It is the story of creation, according to the Maya.

ACKNOWLEDGEMENTS

Professor Don Johnson helped me prepare for the trip by sharing his experiences and studies;

South Puget Sound Community College library loaned me the resource books of Mayan anthropology and culture;

The International Committee with Sherrie Buendel gave me the opportunity to present my work to the campus community;

Kathy Morris, editor, held me accountable to get chapters to her each week;

Patrick Cavendish, Penny Flenniken, Barbara Packard, Maitri Sojourner, Larry Stichweh, Sherry Sullivan, Sharon Wallace and **Larry Zessin** read these pages and offered their corrections;

Eric Oderman assisted with technical scans, picture and word placement;

LeeAnn McGarity designed the book layout; and

Barbara Packard gave me the support to see that this book would be published.

I thank them all for their involvement with me to share this story, *Travels to Maya: 14 days in the Yucatán*.

RESOURCES

Adams, James R. (2010). Cahokia Uncovered. *Indian.* Smithsonian. National Museum of the American Indian. Winter, p. 18-27.

Benchwick, Greg. (1985). *Cancun, Cozumel & the Yucatan.* Lonely Planet

Blookgarden, Richard (1982). *The Easy Guide to Chichen Itza, Balankanchen and Izamal.* Forsyth Travel Library, Shawnee Mission, Kansas.

Bopp, Judie, Bopp, Michael, Brown, Lee, and Lane, Phil, Jr. (1984). *The Sacred Tree: Reflections on Native American Spirituality.* Twin Lakes, WI. Lotus Light Publications.

Bordewich, Fergus. (2003). Winter Palace: The first major exhibition devoted to the Incas' fabled cold weather retreat highlights Machu Picchu's secrets. *Smithsonian,* Vol. 11: No. 12, p. 111-115.

Brown, Chip. (2011). Lost City of the Maya. *Smithsonian,* Vol. 42: No. 2, p. 36-49.

Clow, Barbara H. (2007). *The Mayan Code: Time acceleration and awakening the world mind.* Bear and Company. Rochester, VT.

Coe, Michael D. (1992). *Breaking the Maya Code.* New York, NY. Thames and Hudson, Inc.

Coe, William R. (1975). *Tikal: A handbook of the ancient Maya Ruins.* The University Museum, University of Pennsylvania, Philadelphia.

Daehnke, Jon and Funk, Charles. (2005). *Cathlapotle: Catching time's secrets.* U.S. Fish & Wildlife Service Cultural Resources Team, Region 1 Sherwood, Oregon.

Diccionario Maya. (2008). Dante. Merida, Mexico

Editorial Prehispanica. (2009). *Chichen Itza: A practical guide and photo album,* English edition. Direccion general del derecho de autor. Reagistro publico del derecho de autor.

Eilperin, Juliet. (2011). Swimming with Sharks. *Smithsonian.* Smithsonian. com. June, p. 34-40.

Fasquelle, Ricardo A. and Fash, Jr., William. (1989). Copan: A royal Maya tomb discovered. *National Geographic Society*, Washington, D.C., October, p. 481–505.

Freidel, David, Schele, Linda, and Parker, Joy. (1995). *Maya Cosmos: Three thousand years on the shaman's path.* New York, NY. William Morrow and Company, Inc.

Garrett, Wilbur E. (1989). La Ruta Maya, *National Geographic Society*, Washington, D.C., Vol. 176, No. 4, October, p. 424–479.

Gugliotta, Guy, Garrett, Kenneth, and Zouravliov, Vania. (2007). The Maya Glory and Ruin, *National Geographic Society*, NATIONALGEOGRAPHIC. COM/MAGAZINE. August, p. 68–109.

Jakie, J. (1985). Ohio Valley: The making of America. *National Geographic Society*, Washington, D.C.

Lutz, Martha. *Visits to Ohio Mounds.* Vimach Associates.

Men, Hunbatz. (1990). Secrets of Mayan Science/Religion. Bear and Company. Rochester, VT

Men, Hunbatz. (2010). The 8 Calendars of the Maya: The Pleiadian cycle and the key to destiny. Bear and Company. Rochester, VT.

Michel, Genevieve. (1991). *The Rulers of Tikal: A historical reconstruction and field guide to the stelae.* Publicaciones Vista. Guatemala, C.A.

Mink, Claudia Gellman. (1999). *Cahokia: City of the sun.* Cahokia Mounds Museum Society. Collinsville, Illinois.

Popol Vuh in the Mayan Art: The sacred book of the Maya as seen from its artistic manifestations. (2005). Merida, Yucatan, Mexico. Pixel Press.

Sabloff, Jeremy A. (1990). *The New Archaeology and the Ancient Maya.* New York: NY. W.H. Freeman and Company. Scientific American Library.

Schele, Linda and Mathews, Peter. (1999). *The Code of Kings: The language of seven sacred Maya temples and tombs.* New York, NY. Simon and Schuster Touchstone.

Schele, L. and Miller, M.E. (1986). *The Blood of Kings: Dynasty and ritual in Maya art.* George Braziller, Inc. and Kimbell art Museum, Fort worth.

Silberberg, R. (1970). *The Mound Builders.* Athens, Ohio. Ohio University Press.

Subiyaya. (1996). *Tree Teachings: A glimpse of Coast Salish knowledge from a practicing shaman's eye.* Ti tuwaduqutSid Institute. Skokomish Tribal Center. Shelton, WA.

University of Chicago Spanish Dictionary. (1987). University of Chicago Press, Chicago.

Young, Barbara. (2013). *The Tree Is Medicine: Stories stemming from the Infant Mortality at the Shoalwater Bay.* Olympia, WA. Self published, limited.

Zorich, Zach. (2009). The Man under the Jaguar Mountain: A new royal Maya tomb emerges from the tunnels beneath Copan's acropolis. *Archaeology.* September/October, p. 38-42.

ABOUT THE AUTHOR

Visiting ancient monuments and studying people of communities beyond her own borders has always fascinated this author. Walking among the Mayan ruins of the Yucatán was an extension of a far earlier visit to another ancient monument—Serpent Mound—in her own back yard of Southern Ohio. She was taken there by her mother when she was four years old and now seeks to understand the spiritual connection between the Maya of the Yucatán and the Mound Builders of the Mississippi Valley. Returning from Peace Corps Volunteer service in Brazil and traveling by bus, boat, and train across South America, she slept high in the Andes Mountains among the ancient ruins of Macho Picchu. Travelling to Beijing to present a workshop for students of the Nurse Training School at the University of Beijing, she walked on the road within the Great Wall of China. From each travel experience, Barbara gleans the lessons to be learned and then applies what she has learned to the resolution of modern day problems.

A welcome to the Mayan Riviera